John Cobb's

CHAPELIKONS

Biblical Meditations
on Living the Spiritual Life
in the Modern World

John Patrick Cobb

and

William Y. Penn, Jr.

TREATY OAK PUBLISHERS

The Chapel Installation

Laity Lodge, Kerrville, TX

photo by Rice Jackson

The Chapel Installation

Laity Lodge, Kerrville, TX

photo by Rice Jackson

PUBLISHER'S NOTE

IKONS
by
John Patrick Cobb

MEDITATIONS
by
William Y. Penn, Jr., and John Patrick Cobb

Copyright © 2020
by John Patrick Cobb and William Y. Penn, Jr.
www.JohnCobb-Artist.com
Cover design by Kimberly Greyer
Frontispiece photos by Rice Jackson

Published and printed in the United States of America

TREATY OAK PUBLISHERS

ISBN: 978-1-943658-43-5

:
Cover Art
detail of *Mary as a Child* (mirror image)

DEDICATION

To Jesus the Christ,
The Son and Lamb of God,
Who takes away the sin of the world.

"…yet mercy triumphs over judgment."

Epistle of James 2:13b

The most magnificent and sacred treasure
we shall encounter in this world
is the human soul

filled with faith, love and kindness.

Fr. Arseny
Russian Orthodox priest and art historian,
whose vibrant, hope-filled faith was refined in the fire
of nineteen years of imprisonment
in Stalin's Gulag Archipelago from 1939-1958

TABLE OF CONTENTS

INTRODUCTION   1

IKONS and MEDITATIONS   35

GROUP I
The Baptismal Triptych

1 - John the Baptist   36

2 - Baptism by Water   50

3 - Baptism by Fire   90

GROUP II
Biblical Figures and Themes

4 - Mary as a Child   98

5 - Ms. Rose: *An Ikon of Christ*   102

6 - Manger and Sacrifice: 104
     Room Between Heaven and Earth

7 - Holy Family Beneath a Tent   110

8 - Jesus Falls the 3rd Time: 116
     9th Station of the Cross

9 - Lifting Up On the Cross   120

10 - Taking Down From the Cross: 124
       13th Station of the Cross

11 - The Seen and The Unseen   126

12 - St. Peter's Prayer of Repentance   132

13 - Nathanael   138

GROUP III
Saints in the Church

14 - St. Francis and Br. Leo   142

15 - Our Lady of Guadalupe   152

16 - El Santo Niño: *The Holy Child*   154

GROUP IV
The Human Journey Into Goodness

17 - Ministry to the Widow and Orphan   158

18 - Machismo and Filial Piety   160

19 - Joy: *My Brother in Law, Jesse Serano*   164

20 - Eternal Life: *Br. Andrew, CSC*   168

21 - The Record Taker: *Br. Jeremiah, CSC*   170

22 - Faith and Reason   174

23 - Elder Dressed in White and Wearing
     a Golden Crown   176

24 - The Final Vows of Sister Mary Theodore   180

25 - Dream of the Friend   182

POSTSCRIPT   191

SELECTED BIBLIOGRAPHY   192

ABOUT THE ARTIST   194

ABOUT THE AUTHOR   196

ACKNOWLEDGEMENTS   198

INTRODUCTION

William Y. Penn, Jr.

1.

BEGINNINGS

John Cobb and I began our friendship in 1980, forty years ago. I was teaching Theology and Philosophy at St. Edward's University in Austin, Texas, and he took one of my courses. We kept in touch over the years, even after I retired from St. Edward's in 1999. I have long admired his artistic craftmanship and deep sense of personal vocation as an iconographer and a landscape and portrait artist. We would visit in his home and studio, often speaking together about his work and the spiritual aspirations that fuel it.

He also has remarkable construction skills. He built the home where he and his wife Tina, and her severely handicapped brother, Jesse, now live. Jesse is featured in the ikon *Joy,* and the meditation focuses on his history in the life of the family and the joy he brings to everyone in the household. John initially built the house many years ago for his mother. She was a high school teacher of English and journalism. She was also the original developer of "The Alternative Educational Program" in Texas.

It seems John is always involved in constructing something, whether replacing the septic system on his three-acre place on the east side of Austin near the Colorado River, remodeling a bedroom for Jesse, piecing together frames for his artwork, rebuilding a porch or wall, and improving and refining the traveling Chapel.

About ten years ago he asked me to write meditations on some of his ikons then on display in the central office of the Catholic Diocese of Austin. I attended the exhibit with him by my side. I thoroughly enjoyed it, but was still largely clueless about the depth of the ikons' spiritual meanings. I asked him to talk to me about the ikons and his thought processes when painting them. What he shared opened my eyes and I understood what I needed to write. Sometimes it took only a few words from him and I grasped the spiritual meanings written in paint on that ikon.

One of the most dramatic examples is his ikon *Manger & Sacrifice (Room Between Heaven and Earth)*. Because we had both worked in Ag and with cattle, I was entranced by his luminous depiction of cows. He told me the general story of how the ikon came to be, and then one day when I was again admiring that ikon on the wall of his home, John made the brief comment:

> *Working on that ikon taught me the primitive meaning of sacrifice.*

It was all I needed to hear. Just those few words enabled me to understand the rich spiritual themes written in paint on the carefully prepared "board" that became the ikon. In our walk together through his exhibit, he shared the spiritual themes he was "writing" in egg tempera and gold leaf. I then began the writing process that resulted in the first seven or eight meditations.

Then in the summer of 2018, he mailed me a binder with photos of all twenty-five ikons he exhibits in many parts of the country in his Traveling Ikon Chapel. A two-month exhibit was planned, beginning in December of 2018 at Mexic-Arte Gallery on South Congress Avenue in downtown Austin. He asked if I would do a complete set of Meditations for all of them.

Out of this effort we also began a search for a publisher experienced with formatting fine art and the accompanying texts in an electronic format globally available on the internet. A close friend of John's, Ginger Geyer, an art expert and important supporter of his vocation as an artist over many years, introduced us to Cynthia Stone. Cynthia is owner of Treaty Oak Publishers in Austin and specializes in indie publishing for a variety of writers and artists. Her expert, patient, and caring guidance skillfully led us through the process. It took me two years to complete the additional research, writing, and revisions. I believe this material is necessary to assist viewers of John's *Ikons* to a deeper discovery of the spiritual richness hidden within these luminous, biblically-based images depicting the concrete reality of living the spiritual life in the modern world.

2.

KINDRED SOULS

I am a generation older than John and we have very different personalities. But there are important commonalities. We have both done, and thoroughly enjoy, physically demanding agricultural labor working with cattle. We both were drawn to active, adventuresome outdoor challenges. John became a skilled surfer, beginning with smaller waves on the Gulf Coast of Texas, then moving on to bigger challenges in Mexico, California, and Hawaii. He has an amazing story of an encounter with a great white shark while on his surfboard in big waves in a large lagoon on the coast of Mexico.

I found my adventures working with horses, pack animals, and cattle in my teens and early twenties on my parents Guest Ranch and Wilderness outfitting business in Colorado. There was nothing I loved more than riding a strong, energetic, sure-footed cow horse, rounding up wild cattle in rugged, high mountain country.

But these adventuresome lifestyles proved ultimately unsatisfying to both of us. The physical adrenaline rush involved in riding a narrow board through powerful waves or hot horses chasing wild cattle in rough country, was not sufficient to satisfy the deeper longings of our hearts and minds. We both kept looking for something more.

John studied and worked with art since childhood. This was his principal love affair almost from the beginning. As a young adult he traveled Europe on a Vespa with his backpack, visiting all the great art museums. Then he returned to Austin to enroll in studies in art at St. Edward's University.

When young, I had little discipline or focus and seemed not to have a fire in the belly for anything important beyond my mountain horseback adventures. I had never done well in school. I graduated from high school in 1958 in the bottom 10% of my class. Yet somehow I was accepted into the University of Texas at Austin. There I spent four miserable, and yet strangely fruitful, years wandering among a variety of academic disciplines, first Journalism and then Experimental Psychology and Physical Anthropology.

In part, because of a lack of academic discipline and focus, I succeeded only in making a mess of things, ending up expelled from the university. On the outside, John's personal life trajectory and mine were quite different, his much more focused and disciplined than mine. But as we entered our twenties, the outcome for both of us was identical—a deep and all-consuming cynicism and despair.

John describes the experience in his Bio, and what he writes also described mine, both the experience itself and its underlying cause. It was "an underlying dynamic of duress, a complete despair really, an unseen development of a hatred for life and oneself—*all because (we) had no real knowledge of the "Spirit"*.

It was only as real knowledge of the *"Spirit"* began entering our lives that the cancerous growth of emptiness, lack of ultimate meaning, cynicism, and growing despair began to be overcome. The *knowledge* gradually came to birth in John first through his experience of the shared religious life of the Brothers of Holy Cross at St. Edwards. Then it progressively grew as he took up the disciplined spiritual and meditative practice of iconography. He began increasingly to experience the reality of Christ the interior teacher as he did that spiritual work and sought more and more daily to live deeper by the teachings of the Gospels.

Real knowledge of the "Spirit" came to me in more dramatic and sudden ways, perhaps because the Lord saw me in more desperate need of help than John. When I turned twenty, my depression and despair grew life-threatening. Two things kept me from ever fatally giving up. The first was the deep love of my parents for one another and for my brother and myself. For all my personal limitations, I was determined not to do something that would bring unspeakable tragedy and grief upon them.

The second was my first experience at the age of eight or nine of *the Light from on High* that often plays such a powerful role in lasting moral and religious conversions. I will speak more at length about that in Section 10 of this Introduction on medically researched *Near Death Experiences* (NDEs).

At the heart of John's and my collaboration is the quest for *real knowledge of the "Spirit"* and the desire to share it. It often surprises us the regularity with which we both come to the same basic insights into how "the Spirit" is at work in our world. It is especially surprising given that we reach these similar insights while working separately and doing the intellectual and spiritual work in dramatically different mediums.

John works in the medium of images using egg tempera and gold leaf to represent what he has discovered. I did my work as a scholar and teacher of ancient and modern philosophical and religious texts. Most of my published research was in moral development. Yet we both were reaching very similar conclusions about what it means to live an authentic spiritual life in the modern world.

This is why I often was able, after only a few words of explanation from John, to examine his ikon images and write several pages of meditation about them with little or no additional discussion. While I always checked with him to see if my verbal interpretation was correct, his response, almost always, was a big smile and a "thumbs up".

While our insights were often similar, we also found them enriched and further developed by one another's work in the very different symbolic mediums of images and words.

This synergy of word and image is the living heart of this book. We are both convinced that what each of us has devoted our lives spiritually to sharing with others in our own chosen medium is now shared more effectively by combining these two distinct mediums than can be achieved by either images or words alone.

3.

THE JOURNEY

We both regard the spiritual life as a journey; it is progressive, not regressive, and never static. It is like riding a bicycle. The scene surrounding you is ever changing. If you stop pedaling and moving forward, you fall over.

But what are we moving towards? Things get unsettled and confusing; we take a terrible fall; we experience tragedy and suffering that seem impossible to bear. How are we to discern whether anything we do makes sense and whether our lives are in fact moving in a positive direction?

We do not believe in easy or formulaic answers. The goal of the soul's journey cannot be described as a physical state. It is a condition of faith, enlightenment, love, and mercy, which constitute the interior and exterior state of all who are spiritually willing and able to enjoy the divine grace that the divine spirit freely offers.

> "The only way to God is through doing good, through helping others and denying the enormous human 'I' we are always trying to push forward."
>
> *(Fr. Arseny 1893-1973,* p. 186)

The most important pathways we've discovered that lead to enduring joys are disclosed in the choices we've made about how to live. They are not found simply in works of art or books and ideas, though all of these can help us discover different possibilities for living that we can interpret however we choose. Only when we *act* on them, not just think about or imagine them, do they become real and concrete. When Christianity is reduced to beautiful words, pictures, music, and buildings, it descends into a terrible, anesthetizing, destructive delusion.

John and I approach this task as Catholic Christians with a deeply grounded biblical orientation. But we also recognize that there are many other paths that lead people to a deep grasp of the reality of living an authentic spiritual life in the modern world. We seek especially through the final ikon "Dream of the Friend" and the meditation on a poem by Rumi, the Muslim Sufi mystic and poet, to point to common and sharable features in all authentic spiritualities of whatever religion or none that foster the essential religious values of love, mercy and sacrifice.

All of the Chapel Ikons are meditations on what we encounter again and again in the Bible—dramatic stories of individuals, many of whom were not members of the Jewish faith, seeking a positive path through the storms and struggles of life. In each case, a deep individual conversion was required, one that transcended the established, yet distorted, conventions of prevailing tribal norms and authoritarian religious institutions. The account of Jesus' interaction with a Roman Centurion in Capernaum provides an illustration of Jesus' freedom from the cultural hostilities and institutionalized religious blinders of the religious authorities of his time. (*Matthew 8:5-13*)

The Centurion comes to him beseeching healing for a beloved slave "lying paralyzed" and "in terrible distress" at his home. The Centurion is not only a non-Jew and a foreigner, but he is also a commander of military forces the Jewish people considered hateful agents of oppression. Jesus responded with compassion and healed the slave whom the Centurion deeply loved.

Jesus marveled at this outsider's—a hated foreigner—positive response to his person and message, even before his beloved slave was healed. To those around him Jesus said,

> "Truly, I say to you, not even in Israel have I found such faith.
> I tell you, many will come from east and west and sit at table
> with Abraham, Isaac, and Jacob in the kingdom of heaven,
> while the sons of the kingdom will be thrown into the outer
> darkness; there men will weep and gnash their teeth."
> *(Matthew 8:10-12)*

Jesus is presented in the New Testament as positively engaged with a great diversity of people of different ethnic backgrounds and beliefs, as well as desperate needs. His message had broad spiritual reach, applicable to all, both within and outside his own Jewish faith community. The moralistic and judgmental religious conventions of his time did not constrain Jesus. We find light and encouragement in the Gospel stories of the struggles and hopes of ordinary people, including outsiders such as the Roman Centurion or the Samaritan woman at the well, whom Jesus encountered and affirmed. Jesus associated with prostitutes and tax collectors.

The religious authorities considered his behavior a moral and religious scandal. In contrast, Jesus viewed his actions as flowing from his obedience to the most important of God's commandments—*love of God and love of neighbor.*

John and I are both enlightened and encouraged by the New Testament authors' honest disclosures of the substantial weaknesses and slowness of understanding of Jesus' teachings even by the innermost circle of his chosen Apostles. This helps us to address our own shortcomings and lack of comprehension with more patience and compassion. Equally important is the witness the New Testament provides, in spite of the Apostles many weaknesses and failings, of the multiple ways they still were able to keep on a positive path to an ever more inclusive and compassionate goodness.

An example is the ikon on Peter's prayer of repentance. This key figure in the New Testament has taken a terrible fall on life's journey, betraying everything he believed truly important. And Peter was not alone in this. Both he and Judas betrayed a sacred trust, but Peter was able to turn inward and find a positive way forward. Judas also turned inward and found only a path to self-destruction. In the meditation on this ikon, we explore what we believe helped Peter to regain his balance, then to rise up again on a remarkably positive path, and what led Judas to choose instead the path of self-hatred and suicide.

Through the synergy of images and words, we seek to imagine and explore the positive applications of these biblical stories to our world today. What do they teach that gives us hope, helps us maintain our inner spiritual balance and discern what we must do to keep our lives moving forward in positive ways?

In Jesus' message, person, and struggles, and in the struggles of those he served, we encounter the light that illumines our path.

4.

ST. BONAVENTURE'S
JOURNEY INTO GOODNESS

St. Bonaventure, whom the church refers to as "the seraphic doctor," was a 13th century theologian, Franciscan, and spiritual writer. He was also a Bishop and Minister General of the "Little Brothers," the preferred self-designation of the members of St. Francis' religious community.

Bonaventure describes the three essential movements of the soul's journey in helpful ways. His description offers broad conceptual reach, applicable both to the ancient and modern worlds, and to anyone committed to a spiritual life. Its general application does not require any specific religious beliefs. It does, however, require the conviction that a fruitful spiritual life must have a positive moral core, a broad perspective that takes seriously our responsibilities both to others and to ourselves. It also requires a deep passion and burning commitment to keeping our lives moving forward in positive ways.

Bonaventure believed it is the illumined workings of the human conscience that generates the required perspective. He did not regard the moral conscience as something primarily guided by moral rules or a set of religious pre- or proscriptions. At its deepest level, he understood the human conscience as the natural God given attraction of the soul towards an ever-greater goodness.

The nurture of that natural longing in the human soul requires the daily discipline of living a morally responsible life. Any attempt to move forward in the spiritual life apart from this soon becomes corrupt. Instead of a life enabling the sharing of goodness in our world, we see a life destructive both of self and others.

St. Bonaventure describes three essential spiritual movements:

1) From what is less to what is more important.
2) From the exterior to the interior.
3) From what is temporary and passes away to what is eternal.

The dynamic interdependency of these three spiritual movements is central to all the meditations. Every ascent to a higher and more inclusive stage of the spiritual life is constituted when we break free from fixations on:

1) what is not most important,
2) what hinders the development of our interior spiritual capacities for knowledge, love, and mercy, and
3) a fixation on external things and arrangements that always prove temporary.

It is the journey from what is outside of us to what is within, consummating in the soul's ascent into what is above.

5.

CONNECTIONS WITH CLASSICAL GREEK AND RUSSIAN ICONOGRAPHY

Ikons are sacred images that can inspire and strengthen us in the journey towards human goodness and the positive life in community it entails. The Greek term from which the English term "icon" is derived, is *eikos*, meaning image. The standard English dictionary definitions list a variety of meanings, ranging from an object of uncritical religious devotion to a graphic symbol on a computer screen representing objects, apps, or general functions.

We chose the spelling "ikon" (which reflects classical Greek orthography rather than modern English) to emphasize that John's "ikons" have a very different meaning than the usual English definitions and usages of the term.

The Christian tradition of iconography has its beginnings in the earliest centuries of the church. Never a purely artistic or aesthetic enterprise, above all it is a spiritual exercise, rooted and grounded in prayer with the intent to place oneself in the presence of the *"Spirit"*.

> Spiritually inspired ikons can help to restore hope to those oppressed by sorrow and sadness, those who almost lost faith in human justice. They can remind us that there is another life, free from horror and fear, from blood and the evil of this world. When painted with the help of God, such ikons reach out to us and call us, giving us the hope of salvation.
>
> (paraphrase of *Fr. Arseny, 1893-1973*, p 128)

The Greek and Russian traditions follow a more rigorously imposed style than in the West. To emphasize a timeless transcendence distinct from the constantly changing physical world as we know it, they are usually two- rather than three-dimensional. They do not describe the process by which ikons come to be as "painting." Instead they speak of "writing" ikons because they are understood as expressing the timeless spiritual meanings of the words of the Lord and the saints through graphic rather than verbal representations.

The sacred images or "ikons" that come to birth in this process are believed to transcend the natural capabilities of the work of human hands and imagination. Their composition requires a human heart, a creative vision, and a mind fully open to the divine presence and touched and guided by it.

When a truly open-hearted spiritual "reader" comes into the presence of a truly "sacred image," the encounter can provoke a deep personal experience of inexpressible beauty and unearthly glory. It gives the viewer, if you will, a warm and heavenly embrace that transcends all the dreadful turmoil, conflict, and violence of this world. The sacred image then becomes a source of peace and reconciliation even in the midst of a world in which these are distressingly absent. This experience increases our trust, as Shakespeare put it, that

> *There is a divinity that shapes our ends*
> *rough hew them how he will.*

Like the ancient Eastern Christian Orthodox "writers of ikons," with intensive prayer focused on the biblical and spiritual, John crafts his compositions in the classic mediums of egg tempera and gold leaf. It takes exceptional patience, skill, and craftmanship to use egg tempera and gold leaf well. The smaller individual panels take a year or more to complete; a large panel, such as *Baptism by Fire*, takes three years.

Through the ikons, both John and the ancient ikon artists explore and make manifest the transcendent mystery and goodness imbuing all human life and creation.

6.

THE RENAISSANCE AND MODERN CONNECTIONS

What makes John's art distinct from Byzantine iconography are the artistic techniques he uses to manifest the transcendent mystery underlying the complicated, three-dimensional, messy, nitty-gritty realities of our daily lives.

He depicts the mystical path, drawing upon the three-dimensional perspectives developed by European Renaissance painters of the 14th -16th Centuries. Two themes are characteristic of the dramatic cultural shifts of the Renaissance.

First is the intense empirical interest in the natural world as it is. The second is its human focus. Both of these emphases are central to John's work.

With the precision of Renaissance painters, John describes in paint the material reality of his subjects: physical objects that surround or shelter them, living creatures, fabrics, colors and folds in a garment, the play of light and shadows over physical forms. He crafts physical features of faces, eyes, and the direction of a glance and postures to bring out the psychological depth and inner complexity of his subjects.

He refined these gifts in his early twenties during an extended journey to Europe with a backpack and a Vespa. He filled his black sketchbook with watercolors of scenes that caught his eye. Spending long hours in European art museums, he toured for nine months, six in Spain. He speaks of the journey as enabling him to learn much "that the controlled nature of college could not reveal."

7.

A PERSONAL JOURNEY
WITH THE
TRAVELING IKONS

Ginger Geyer's article "Art on Board," in the 2005 fall issue of *Image: Art, Mystery, and Faith*, explores many of the connections between Cobb's work and the European masters. The cover features John's ikon of Mary as a child on a pony and refers to his works as *John Cobb Paints His Neighbors*. She sees John's techniques as classical, though "the result reveals a blend of influences."

His favorite religious painter is Rembrandt. When she asked John how he chose his subjects, he told her he looks for the tenderness expressed in Rembrandt's Jewish Bride—"a painting he reveres so much that he can barely speak about it."

John also draws inspiration from the Spanish artists Velasquez and Goya, and the American artists Peter Hurd, famous for his paintings of the American West, and Hurd's father-in-law, Andrew Wyeth.

Ginger writes of an intriguing episode when she helped John move his ikons from his cramped and cluttered upstairs studio at his home in East Austin near the Colorado River into an enclosed rental truck. It is a luminous personal account, not only of the beauty of John's work, but also of John.

The ikons and chapel were transported to an exhibit at the H.E. Butt Laity Lodge exhibit center nestled in the Frio River Canyon of Central Texas. She was art consultant to Laity Lodge.

Ginger shares a fascinating tale of helping John load and lash the pieces of his traveling chapel in which he displays the ikons onto a rusty beat up trailer with bare tires and out-of-date license plates, pulled by his well-used Mazda pick-up.

Then she and her husband set off with John "like the Israelites into the wilderness with our tabernacle on a flatbed…"

8.

A TRANSFORMING SPIRITUAL DISCOVERY

The critical period in John's progressive journey both as artist and messenger was his arrival at St. Edward's University and the deep friendships he developed with the Brothers of Holy Cross.

As he writes in his biography, his time in Europe ended when he ran out of money. Then he returned to Austin to embrace his parents' wishes, pursuing his eventual degree in art from St. Edward's University, an institution founded by the Catholic religious community of Holy Cross.

John writes of the positive spiritual impact of the Brothers of Holy Cross, both on him as a person and on his art. As he shares below, his paintings of the Chapel Ikons and what they convey is very much inspired by their spirituality. The Brothers' ways of living and relating to people helped him to develop a new concept of "believing." Six members of the religious community of Holy Cross are depicted in his ikons.

The ikons also express the importance of a sense of responsibility for self and for others. John sees this awareness of personal responsibility as rooted in two distinct but interrelated phenomena. The first is the development of an objective knowledge of the 'Spirit'. The second is a grounding in a spiritual community which further strengthens and develops that knowledge.

What I really discovered while at St. Edward's was that I had no real knowledge of the *"Spirit."* Oh, maybe Robert Henri's "Art Spirit," but no perception beyond my own understanding.

A new concept of believing led to an overwhelming need to be responsible, for myself, and for others.

My parents' divorce, my own propensity to embrace existentialism (an earlier grappling with Camus' despairing novel, *A Happy Death in Morocco).* led to an underlying dynamic of duress, a complete despair really, an unseen development of a hatred for life and oneself—all because I had no real knowledge of the *"Spirit."*

The Brothers at St. Ed's revealed to me more positive options. I sensed the possibility of a grounding in a spiritual community.With that, I began this egg tempera series, seeking to generate a sequence of works flowing from ancient traditions and moving towards the here and now and the ever new.

My goal is to take what is sacred and to hold it steadfast, while moving forward in ways that no degree of malfeasance could defeat.

9.

INDIVIDUAL SPIRITUAL CREATIVITY AND TRUST IN DIVINE PROVIDENCE

Our intention is not to limit the free and creative spiritual imaginations of our readers to any specific interpretation we share in these meditations. We hope to encourage their independent and imaginative spiritual creativity. Like water from a fountain many fruitful "spiritual readings" flow from these ikons, as varied as the different individuals viewing them.

The life of the divine presence in our souls accompanies each person down diverse and very different roads. The diversity of individual life experiences and needs inevitably leads to different interpretative frameworks. In order to encourage individual viewers to use their own imaginations and reach their own interpretations, we make no effort to interpret every aspect of an ikon.

Central to our Christian faith is the belief that God created each of us in the image of the divine freedom, creativity, and love. God did not create us in the likeness of a programmable computer. The Spirit calls each of us to participate in the creative works of divine wisdom in free and truly collaborative ways. Our constricted religious imaginations often find this difficult to conceive.

John envisions his ikons as ways of expanding the envelope. What is most important is that each of us, whether believers or not, may find and be faithful to his or her own individual and freely chosen paths to a more thoughtful, compassionate, peaceful and fruitful spiritual life. The possibility of new spiritual life calls each of us to be engaged in the three most important movements of that life—moving, day by day, from what is less to what is more important, from the exterior to the interior, and from what passes away to what is everlasting.

John and I understand the Christian faith as affirming that in the end only two things are required to enter heaven. First, we must be willing to accept God's forgiveness of our own sins—all the ways we think or act that are destructive or diminish what is truly good. Second, we must be willing to forgive others their sins against us. Often what is most important is what we are able to accept, not what we are able to do. This in every case and above all is the acceptance of God's universal mercy.

This most ancient of Christian beliefs, explicit in the Lord's Prayer, is clearly articulated in the spiritual writings of many of the greatest saints, for example the 14th century Catherine of Siena and the 16th century Teresa of Avila. At the heart of this faith is the conviction that the power of God's mercy is infinitely greater than all human cruelty and destructiveness, in the world, in the church and in every religion, from the very beginning of human history to its very end.

10.

NDE'S:
NEAR DEATH EXPERIENCES

Some of the first and most important modern empirical research into these experiences by medical professionals was published by Dr. Raymond Moody in 1973 in his book, *Life After Life*. He has interviewed hundreds of patients who recount these experiences. He provides a brief description of the common elements most frequently present in these accounts.

A man is dying and, as he reaches the point of greatest physical distress, he hears himself pronounced dead by his doctor. He then hears an uncomfortable noise, a loud ringing or buzzing, and at the same time feels himself moving, very rapidly through a long dark tunnel. After this he suddenly finds himself outside of his own physical body, but still in the same physical environment, as though he is a spectator. He watches the resuscitation attempts from this unusual vantage point and is in a state of emotional upheaval...

He notices that he still has a "body," but one with very different powers from the physical body he has left behind...

Others come to meet him and to help him. He glimpses the spirits of relatives and friends who have already died, and a loving warm spirit of a kind he has never encountered before—a being of light—appears before him. This being asks him a question, nonverbally, to make him evaluate his life and helps him along by showing him a panoramic, instantaneous playback of the major events of his life... He is overwhelmed by intense feelings of joy, love, and peace. Despite his attitude, though, he somehow reunites with his physical body and lives. (*21-23*)

When these individuals attempt to share the experience with others, they cannot find words for it. And many people quickly dismiss it all as a weird hallucination. So they cease attempting to share it. But the experience profoundly affects how they live in the future and dramatically changes "(their) views about death and its relation to life."

The most important changes are that these individuals are no longer afraid of dying and there is a dramatic change in what they now consider the two most important priorities in life:

1) Learning to love other people and
2) growing in knowledge and understanding.

They often give extraordinarily accurate and detailed reports of the complicated medical procedures and conversations going on around them even as they were pronounced "dead" by their physicians. Even had they been fully conscious, they could not have observed from their physical location on the emergency treatment table or bed all that was going on around them. They also report conversations and activities occurring in their homes distant from the hospital where they were treated. These reports were verified as accurate by medically trained researchers.

How they could have acquired this knowledge seems impossible to explain unless they had in fact been "out of their bodies". To many, this is convincing evidence that we do possess a mind or soul able to be fully conscious and aware, independent of the body.

But many of the medical researchers, including Raymond Moody, who was trained both in medicine and philosophy, do not consider these accounts solid scientific proof. However, many of them who initially did not believe that we have "souls" that can exist independently of our bodies, now "believe" that that we do. This includes Dr. Moody.

I agree with Moody. My own studies in the Philosophy of Science and Logic lead me to a similar conclusion, though more forcefully stated: The rigorously empirical and quantitative methodologies of modern science and its basic underlying assumptions about the kind of realities it is researching and how to research them, render any scientific proof of the reality of the supernatural logically impossible. Religious faith in the supernatural takes us beyond what our physical eyes can see, and requires different ways of approaching reality than the methods available to modern science. No one has expressed this more succinctly than Albert Einstein:

> For the scientist, there is only "being," but no wishing, no valuing, no good, no evil; no goal. As long as we remain within the realm of science proper, we can never meet with a sentence of the type: "Thou shalt not lie ..." ...Scientific statements of facts and relations, indeed, cannot produce ethical directives."
>
> (*Out of My Later Years*, p. 114)

To understand the transcendent moral reality, beyond what we empirically encounter in this world, requires the development of different spiritual ways of seeing and understanding than the empirical and quantitative methods of modern science. This is in no way to discount the critical importance of modern science. It is key to human survival. Only there can we learn how most effectively to deal with death-dealing diseases, the most efficient ways to produce food and energy not destructive to our planet, and so many other things important to a more broadly sharable human flourishing on earth.

But science also places in our hands vast powers that can bring to an end all vertebrate life on our planet. The factual knowledge that science provides can equally promote a wonderous human flourishing but also can readily lead to the unleashing of unimaginably horrendous forces of destruction, ending all conscious life on our planet.

For the good to prevail, we need more than science. We need sound ethics and authentic, healthy and deeply moral and spiritual ways of understanding and living. We desperately need a positive, humble, and respectful partnership between the sciences and the authentic spiritualities available in every religion. I also believe that these spiritual ways of seeing and understanding are based no less on actual human experience than is the scientific enterprise. But they are very different kinds of experiential certification than those sought in rigorously scientific methods. Those who have experienced them (including many scientists) often become convinced that these experiences reveal the eternal reality of "the Spirit" which created the universe and gives to our lives eternal meaning, both moral and spiritual, that does not end with our physical deaths. The NDE research has much of importance to teach us about this.

A decade after Moody's book was published, Dr. Melvin Morse began researching reports of this same kind of experience by children, some as young as four. Morse is the author of the Seattle Study, carried out by a research team of medical experts on the Near Death Experiences of children. His work is a remarkable supplement to the work of Moody and many other researchers in this field. It is published in his book: *Closer to the Light: Learning from the Near Death Experiences of Children.*

Morse, previous to this study, did mainstream medical research on the effects of radiation therapy on a child's brain.

As a result of his Near Death studies, Morse now firmly believes in what the ancients knew:

> All must die and death is not to be feared. There is a Light that we all will experience after death and that Light represents joy, peace, and unconditional love. (*197*)

What has most impressed me about the research is the remarkable and enduring impact of the experience of "the being of light" upon how these individuals subsequently live their lives. Morse provides an eloquent summary of the permanently life changing impact upon individuals after their encounter with "the Light". The individual experiences reveal:

> more love and caring than he had ever felt from anyone on earth, the master Being of Light engulfs him with his presence, taking him on a multi-dimensional view of his life. Not only does he see everything he has done to everybody, but he feels everything as well. *Not only does he experience how he felt when it happened, he knows how it felt to the other person.* This sensory barrage is accompanied by a moral commentary from the Being of Light who compassionately communicates to the person what he did right and wrong and indicates things he might do in the future.

> The problem is the person wants this experience to go on forever. He doesn't want to leave the Being of Light's bosom. He tells this to the being, but he is given no choice. He must return. (*11*)

These individuals return to their bodies transformed. Their previously selfish, materialist and ego-centered lives are now replaced by "a thirst for knowledge, feelings, and expressions of love that astonishes the people that knew (them)." (*11*)

It is not, however, necessary to have an NDE to see the Light. Morse shares the report of Oxford scholar Edwin Robinson of his spiritual experience of the Light as a four-year-old. This report is especially moving to me because of its similarity to my own first experience of the Light as a child of eight or nine.

> My mother and I were walking on a stretch of land known locally as the moors. As the sun declined and the slight chill of the evening came on, a pearly mist formed over the ground. Suddenly I seemed to see the mist as a shimmering gossamer tissue and flowers appearing here and there, seemed to shine with a brilliant fire. Somehow I understood that this was the living tissue of life itself, in which what we call consciousness was embedded appearing here and there was a shining focus of energy in that more diffused whole. In that moment I knew that I had my own special place, as had all other things.
>
> The vision has never left me, and with it the same intense feeling of love for the world and the certainty of ultimate good. (*143-144*)

I also had a similar vision of the Light as a child on a remarkable walk. I was not with my mother but alone. I was not in an open moor in the countryside but on a sidewalk on Storey St. in my neighborhood in Midland, Texas. Neighborhood homes stretched out before and behind me on both sides of the street. On my left was a large vacant lot.

Suddenly everything exploded into Light, a Light unlike anything I had ever before experienced. As an adult I still have no words adequate to describe it. But it was a Light clearly communicating to me that my life had a meaning and purpose, "that I had my own special place, as had all other things" and a certainty that "an ultimate goodness" was at work in the world.

In that brief moment I experienced a peace and joy unlike anything I had ever experienced. That experience has never left me. I feel it as vividly today as I did over seventy years ago. At the time I did not identify it with anything explicitly religious. It was purely and simply a powerful experience (which at the age of eight I wouldn't even have described as "spiritual") that my life had a meaning and purpose, though what that was to be was in no way indicated.

I was raised in a deeply loving and responsible family, though it was not a family with any practice of prayer or openly expressed religious faith. My parents were nominal Presbyterians who seldom attended a church service.

After this experience of the Light I walked home, just a block away, feeling like I was walking on air. My father was seated at our breakfast room table. I sat down beside him and attempted to communicate something of the powerful and mysterious experience I just had. He listened, but it was clear it didn't make any sense to him. So I dropped it and have never previously shared it except with a very few very close friends.

A few months after I turned twenty, I was to have a second experience of the Light, this time religiously focused, and forever altering how I choose to live. An older friend who knew of my drinking problems invited me to attend a talk at an AA meeting given by a woman named Gertrude Behanna. She had suffered over decades the ravages of alcoholism, three broken marriages, and multiple suicide attempts.

After her very nearly successful and final effort at suicide, she regained consciousness in a hospital room with an IV tube in her arm. What she discovered patiently waiting for her was utterly unexpected. She describes the experience in her life's story, *The Late Liz*, written under the pseudonym Elizabeth Burns:

> In the flow of eternal time there is one certain period in which time seems to rest, to hold its breath before mustering forces for the reversal from dark to light, from ebb to flow. It is then that mankind is prone to slip most easily out from this phase of life over into the next phase. This is not a break, an hiatus, but rather a slender swaying bridge between what is here and what is somewhere else…
>
> A faint light was beyond the curtains, so far beyond that it was more the suggestion of light than light. And there was no sound at all. The world in which I lay was a very private world and I was quite alone. And then, all at once, I was not alone.

Throughout the whole of existence there are a few, a very few things which are true and which one accepts as true and this was one of them. I was not alone. Something was here that had not been here before, it was not a person and not the memory of anyone or anything. What it was I didn't know, merely that it was.

There was no increase in light. No sound. No motion. No scent. Though in a fashion I cannot explain it was all of these, the source of these. Lying utterly still, I waited. Unable to accept, I was now accepting, letting myself be claimed, letting this something mount and permeate and cover the self I'd been as the tide rises to cover what was formerly dry and bare. What it was or where it came from I did not know nor was there any need to know...

This was truth itself and I breathed it into me. The part of man which no man knows stretched out its hands and groped and touched its source and intermingled and flowed back into the place it came from. The soul of me was very, very small, a midget soul, yet, having retained a fraction of its total, it was alive. And so, as it came home, slowly by infinitesimal degrees, the one who was I started to become more than I.

And now, in tremulous fulfillment, I knew what This was, knew and began to tremble. As the plant knows where the light is, I knew.

This was the Father.

My heart trembled. Trembled and swelled until it seemed that it would burst.

How could I... know this? How could I identify the truth of Truth? I cannot answer. I think and think and know that it is so and cannot answer. Behind this, leading up to it, were years of searching and searching and finding what was not-true, and maybe this was a portion of the answer. Maybe finding enough not-truths and never settling for non-truths, brings Truth a little nearer.

The air was radiant with a gladness to burst the heart. An outpouring, drenching and cradling and upholding the person who was I, yet not I. The scant, leftover shred of me, as yet unspoiled, was going back. Back to the One Who has always waited, only now the barrier between had disappeared.

The barrier had been in me. The Father had been here forever; the Circle starting from and ending in Itself; the Source; the Father with a hundred names and no name. And no name needed. This was the Meaning, the Answer to all there was or ever could be. . .

I could think of only one untarnished word. This word was Glory.

Here was the Glory of the Patient Presence Which had waited since the first beginning.

Wonder came. A vast well of overwhelming wonder into which I sank, released. Immediate with the wonder came the peace, not the timed peace the world knows, but an in-going at-oneness. And then, following for one split second, came an actual sense of timelessness. Of a forever.

And I understood. By this I understood that I had been forgiven. That whatever I had been and done, or not been or not done, was forgiven me. Whatever else life held I was being given now a washed page; my tiny soul had all eternity in which to grow. . .

Surely tears ran down my face but if they did, I did not feel them because they had not sprung from sorrow. That would come. I somehow knew, yet for the moment there was no sorrow, no regret, no guilt. Nor were there fears or questions.

Wonder and peace and forgiveness was all that I had room for.

What was to come would come later.

(Chapter 13, pp. 172-177)

There was, however, nothing magical or instantaneous about this. Overcoming her addiction to alcohol was a painful process she had to complete largely on her own, though also aided by divine grace. And once that spiritual battle was completed, she moved forward on her journey to discover the path to a meaningful and stable life in service of others.

My friend thought she might have something to say to me. Since it was clear I could use some help, I said to myself, "Why not?" and went to her talk. It was interesting, tough, earthy, and filled with realism. This intrigued me. Gert set up an appointment with me in "the Black room" at the Episcopal Theological Seminary of the Southwest in Austin. The room was named after a Judge Black who had donated his formal library, walnut paneling, formal furniture, books and all, to the Seminary.

I went to our meeting with all manner of intellectual questions, none of which Gert answered. What her presence did provide was precisely "the answer" I needed, a real experience of the Spirit that could draw me out of the chaos that was my life onto a path that would guide me for the rest of my life into an ever-greater goodness. Gert Behanna was to be God's chosen instrument accomplishing this for me. She did not merely transform my life, she saved it.

I entered the room, shook her hand, and sat down in a chair in that formal walnut panelled library, and suddenly the room exploded into Light, literally bouncing off of the walls, the same Light that I encountered at the age of eight or nine. Only this time it was clearly identified with the name of Jesus and I knew my life would never be the same again.

I don't even recall what Gert and I talked about. It was clear to me that the Light was not coming from her, rather from a source infinitely more powerful than Gert, using her as its chosen instrument. I now knew God was real, Jesus was his instrument at work in the world, and I was called to follow him.

Shortly afterwards my terrible academic performance caught up with me and I was expelled from the University. I entered the US Army and served as a Chaplain's Assistant with the Third Armored Division in Kirchgoens, Germany. After receiving a European discharge, I began formal Theological and Scripture studies at the University of Bonn in Germany. Then I returned to UT to finish my undergraduate degree in Philosophy.

Never before had I ever made an 'A' in a University course, and now I was making straight 'As'. How I gained admission to the prestigious University of Bonn and then into the rigorous PhD program in Philosophy at the University of Texas at Austin, in spite of my academic transcript littered with 'Fs', is itself a book of miracles. For me it was quite like God's parting of the Red Sea to allow his chosen people to pass through in safety during their escape from Egypt.

While completing a dissertation on Soren Kierkegaard, I taught Religion for three years in an inner city Holy Cross High School in Akron, Ohio, and then from there obtained my position in Theology and Philosophy at St. Edward's University back in Austin.

Since that second experience of the *Light from on High*, sixty years ago, my life has never diverged from my central sense of vocation to share with others the transformative power of real knowledge about the work of the all merciful and compassionate Spirit at work in our world.

11.

THE ORGANIZATION OF
THE BOOK

The numbered sequence of ikons in this book of photographic reproductions has never been used in exhibitions of the ikons. This book and these meditations are still a work in process.

The goal is to offer a single volume with photographic reproductions of all the currently complete Chapel Ikons and Meditations. The one-page reproductions are small (measurable in inches) in comparison to the original works (measurable in feet). But they are still able to capture a bit of the richness of color, details, and luminosity of the originals. Most important, they provide a life setting from which the symbolism flows. We felt a need to organize them into an intelligible sequence, like the order of chapters in a book.

Group I - *A Baptismal Triptych*

This includes three different ikons, an ikon on the person of John the Baptist, an ikon on his Baptism of Repentance by Water, and the concluding ikon on Baptism by the Fire of the Holy Spirit.

The account of John's Baptism of Repentance by Water in the desert wilderness of Judea provides the launching pad from which all four Gospels of the New Testament (*Matthew, Mark, Luke and John*), launch their accounts of the trajectory of Jesus' public ministry, passion and resurrection. Because of the importance of this material setting the context for all that follows, it is in the Group I written materials that the reader will find the most extensive documentation and explanatory accounts underlying my meditations on what lies at the core of Jesus' teachings in the Gospels.

It is an understanding prefigured and logically grounded in the Old Testament witness of the law and the prophets, reaching fulfillment only in the radically new teaching of the New Covenant proclaimed in the New Testament.

All of the much shorter and more focused meditations of Groups II-IV are grounded in and flow from this understanding of the Christian history of salvation presented in the Group I materials. The Selected Bibliography provides a list of the principal sources I was actively drawing on over the two-year course of writing these materials. It provides any interested reader the source referred to in all the references in the texts of the meditations.

Group II - *Biblical Figures and Themes*

Persons and events in the New Testament narrative largely in the order in which they emerge in the Gospels. Each person is portrayed by one of John's friends, family or acquaintances.

Group III - *Saints in the Church*

Saints officially honored in the history of the church, each portrayed in the person of a friend, family member, or acquaintance of John.

Group IV - *The Human Journey Into Goodness*

An exploration of central Christian themes in the human journey to goodness that John sees lived out daily around him in the lives of his contemporaries.

John Cobb's

CHΛPEL IKONS

Group I

The Baptismal Triptych

ST. JOHN THE BAPTIST
17" x 17"
1984

ST. JOHN THE BAPTIST

John Cobb's three baptismal ikons—*John the Baptist, Baptism by Water*, and *Baptism by Fire*—form a triptych. This ancient style of religious iconography with three panels is usually hinged together. Though not physically attached, John's three ikons are spiritually integrated into a single unit. They present us with an interdependent progression of two distinct baptisms, beginning with John's Water Baptism of Repentance, and culminating in the Baptism of Fire by the Holy Spirit.

In his "writing" of the ikon of the Baptist, John follows his usual pattern. *He takes ancient and traditional religious themes, depicting them in a thoroughly modern context, to focus on the core and continuing relevance today of the ancient images and messages of the Old and New Testaments.*

John conveys the spiritual vision in his ikons similar to the way Jesus communicates his core teachings by using parables. They present captivating representations of the natural world and human situations. The physical content is easy to see. Understanding and then being able to see the spiritual and moral content is more challenging. Neither the crowds around Jesus, nor even his closest disciples, usually seem "to get it".

John's ikons present a similar challenge. Inspired by Jesus' indirect teaching methods, the ikons present beautiful natural images—pleasurable and fascinating to our eyes. Opening our minds and hearts to understand and see the spiritual and moral message is more personally demanding. Today, just as in the time of the Baptist, few ever seem to get the message. Getting Jesus' message requires radically new and transformative ways of thinking, seeing, feeling, and behaving religiously that continue to be just as violently opposed by "religious" people, and "religious" authorities in the modern world as in the ancient.

His ikon of the Baptist depicts a homeless person, a young man he met on St. John's Avenue, in Austin, Texas. The physical depiction recalls the descriptions in the New Testament of John the Baptist, clothed in camel skins in a desert wilderness by the Jordan river, living on locusts and wild honey. The Baptist's hair shirt is what Elijah, the Old Testament prophet who was his model, also wore.

The physical landscape in the ikon is the confluence of the San Juan and Green rivers in the high rocky deserts in Utah above Lake Powell. Also easy to grasp are the parallels between the rocky and barren landscapes depicted in the ikon and in the Judean desert where John preached.

But what possible spiritual connection does this depiction of a homeless person in Austin have with John the Baptist, preaching a water baptism of repentance, in the wilderness of ancient Judea, two thousand years ago?

John Cobb was not painting a physical likeness of the Baptist, which in any case is impossible. His goal in depicting a homeless man was to inspire the spiritual virtues of mercy and compassion, the same interior virtues that the actual John the Baptist sought to enkindle in his hearers by his preaching of repentance.

Most modern readers understand "repentance" as referring to feelings of guilt, remorse, and shame for wrongful actions; however, in the original Greek New Testament the term used is *metanoia*. Its focus is significantly different. It is derived from the Greek noun *Nous*, referring to *Mind* and the Greek verb *Noein* referring to *Thinking*. These include all higher human intellectual capacities.

Metanoia calls for a human openness and awareness of the need for deep and fundamental shifts in how we prioritize our values and how we choose to live. It profoundly affects not just how we feel, but also how we think about and see the world. When the deep interior transformation of *metanoia* occurs, it profoundly alters how we choose to see and to behave.

The modern English meaning of the term "prophet" is also quite different than the meaning it usually has in the Old and New Testaments. Today when we hear someone referred to as a "prophet," we think immediately of someone able to predict the future. But prophets in the Old and New Testaments were primarily understood as moral teachers, divinely gifted at discerning and moving human hearts and minds. (Cf. *1 Corinthians 14:23-25*) Their primary concern was not to predict the future. It was to waken their listeners' sleeping consciences and inspire them to do what is right rather than what is evil. When there were predictions of the future, as there sometimes were, the focus was usually on the inevitable destructive consequences flowing from evil acts.

The primary focus of the Israelite prophets is not on what most today understand as "religious" activities. Their priorities were justice and mercy. Apart from the foundation these moral virtues provide, "religion" inevitably becomes dishonest, cruel, and corrupt.

> *Speak the truth. Be just, kind, compassionate, humble—not self-absorbed and resentful. Feed the hungry, clothe the naked, shelter the homeless, protect widows and orphans, welcome the stranger and the alien.*

None of the ancient Jewish prophets expressed this more clearly and succinctly than the 8th century B.C. prophet, Micah:

> "What does the Lord require of you but to do justice and love kindness and walk humbly with your God." (*6:8*)

The Gospel of Luke tells us that John the Baptist was raised in the desert. There "he grew and became strong in the spirit, and he was in the wilderness till the day of day of his manifestation to Israel." (3:80) His physical foods were locusts and wild honey. Most important, the Hebrew texts of the ancient Jewish prophets spiritually fed and formed him.

We human beings are largely dominated by our physical appetites and deep-rooted desires to protect ourselves, satisfy our sexual drives, obtain wealth, social status, and power over others. These appetites and cravings are genetically embedded in our biological make up. At one time in the ruthless struggle for the survival of the fittest, these increased the chances for the survival of our species.

Today the situation is very different. Modern science and technology have placed the virtually unlimited power of modern weaponry in our hands that can wipe out not only the human species, but all forms of vertebrate life on our planet. Today, if these primitive urges continue to drive us, we will not survive, we will be destroyed.

The ancient Jewish prophets gave witness to spiritual forms of life that offer human beings increasing freedom from the domination of aggressive biological drives. These primitive drives are the source of much of the physical and social destructiveness at work in our world. This progressive liberation from our biological hard wiring requires a conscious and disciplined turning of our focus from the physical to the moral and the spiritual. The Baptist was demanding this transformation when he preached "repentance".

The New Testament understanding of "repentance" is manifested in the three critical movements of the spiritual life we discussed in Section Four of the Introduction: *St. Bonaventure's Journey to Goodness*. These are the movements:

1) *From what is less to what is more important.*
2) *From the exterior to the interior.*
3) *From what is transient to what is eternal.*

These interior transitions lead to the tangible presence in human lives of humility, patience, kindness, self-control, chastity, freedom from domination by anger, sacrificial generosity for the poor and the vulnerable, welcoming the stranger and alien, and justice for all. These are interior virtues that God calls us to express by how we choose to live. Moving forward on this path is difficult. It demands interior spiritual battles to transcend these biological urges and for us to be steadfast in this journey into a greater and more inclusive good.

Highly institutionalized and conformist religious groups seem especially vulnerable to astonishingly regressive development, moving backwards from the more important to the less, from the interior to the exterior, and from what is enduring to what is transient. With astonishing frequency, all the warnings both in the Old and New Testaments— the spiritual dangers of wealth and the central importance of God's commandments to care for the most needy and vulnerable—are simply tossed aside.

Then it is an easy step to become self-protective, even cruel and rapacious, focusing on our own personal or our favored groups' special interests, no matter the harm and devastation inflicted upon vulnerable others. Alas, we often do it with utterly no qualms of conscience, but with a strong, vindictive and self-righteous spirit, that pretends to find a religious justification for our thoughtless and hardhearted deeds. We respond to criticism of our behavior with anger, resentment, and self-justification. Both mind and heart are slammed shut against any authentic repentance.

The Old Testament prophets' radical moral message was their *condemnation of the great sin of breaking the intimate links that should always be maintained between morality, religion, and politics*. The prophetic understanding of morality was broad and inclusive, radically different than the "moral" thinking of most of their "religious" contemporaries. The prophets focused not on protecting the powerful and wealthy, but on care for the poor, the stranger, the foreigner, and the most defenseless.

Strong criticism of the dominant "religious" and social norms of life generated great hostility and often violence towards the prophets. This was true both among the religious and political authorities of the time as well as among ordinary people. Any moral and spiritual criticism was regarded as outrageous, "unpatriotic", and an utterly unacceptable public attack upon the nation's moral and religious integrity.

But how did it happen that John, growing up in the isolated deserts of Judea, came to possess this understanding of the prophets proclaimed so powerfully in his preaching?

If we accept what the Gospel of Luke tells us, that the Baptist was in fact raised since childhood in the desert, only one explanation seems possible -- *Qumran*. Qumran was a semi-monastic, celibate community, established by members of the radical Jewish sect of the Essenes. In the time of the Baptist and Jesus, the Essenes had a significant religious impact in Palestine. As extreme separatists, they refused to associate even with their fellow Palestinian Jews for fear of being religiously and morally corrupted. They were also known to adopt orphaned children in order to care for them and provide them with them religious education and spiritual formation necessary to assure new life in the Essene communities.

Qumran is located about one mile from the northwestern shore of the Dead Sea. Their library contained the sacred Hebrew texts of the ancient Jewish religious tradition, including the law and the prophets. Of special importance to them was the prophet Isaiah, cited in the Manual of Discipline governing their communities. It refers to the same text from *Isaiah 40:5*, that the Baptist also includes in his preaching, emphasizing God's desire for universal salvation:

> *And the glory of the Lord shall be revealed, and **all flesh shall see it together**, for the mouth of the Lord has spoken.*

The Essenes reverently preserved, copied, and studied the spiritual message in these ancient religious texts. They also practiced ritual washings to symbolize religious and moral purity. It would seem that only at Qumran could the Baptist have acquired the depth of knowledge of the prophets, along with the practice of a water baptism of repentance that grew to become the heart of his ministry and preaching. In 1947 many of the Essene biblical scrolls were discovered, hidden in caves in the cliffs above Qumran. The Dead Sea Scrolls, as they are called today, have provided us the most ancient surviving codices of the Old Testament.

In the Gospel of Luke, we are given an account of the Baptist's preaching. Clearly grounded in the message of the ancient Hebrew prophets, it begins with the requirement "to prepare the way of the Lord." Luke's account concludes with the citation (below) from *Isaiah 40:5*. It states the ultimate religious goal of all mature and morally grounded religious striving. God's salvation is intended for all, not just a select few or one's own favored group. The Baptist believed it impossible to achieve this apart from moral foundations with a universal perspective showing care for all, and especially the most vulnerable. Experiencing first hand the connection between seeing "the salvation of God" and showing active care for the most vulnerable among us is paramount.

> In the fifteenth year of the reign of Tiberius Caesar... the word of God came to John, the son of Zacharia, in the wilderness. And he moved into the region all around the Jordan to preach a baptism of repentance for the forgiveness of sin, as it is written in the book of the sayings of Isaiah the prophet:
>
> "A voice of someone crying out in the desert,
> "Make ready the way of the Lord,
> Make straight paths for him...
> What is crooked must become straight,
> And rough ways made smooth,
> ***Then shall all human beings see the salvation of God."***
>
> *(Luke 3:1-6)*

The Isaiah (referred to as Second Isaiah by biblical scholars) who wrote this text was a member of the exiled Jewish community in Babylon, after Babylon destroyed the city of Jerusalem and its holy Temple in 587 B.C.. He wrote these texts five hundred years before the time of the Baptist. He was the first of the Old Testament prophets clearly and uncompromisingly to express this new understanding of God's mission for Israel. It was no longer to be understood as a nationalist religious mission. It was to be a universal, global, all-inclusive, spiritual mission. God called Israel to reach out to all humankind, not just to the tribes and to the nation of Israel.

> "It is too light a thing that you should be my servant to raise up the tribes of Jacob and to restore the preserved of Israel. I will give you as a light to the nations that my salvation may reach to the ends of the earth."
>
> *(Isaiah 49:6)*

This radically inclusive understanding of the divine purpose must have inspired the Baptist's decision to separate himself from the Qumran community and its narrow sectarian religious perspectives. He formed his own community of disciples in the desert, recruiting those who shared this new and more inclusive religious perspective. Together with his band of disciples, the Baptist responded to God's call *to preach to all of Israel*. The new focus was to prepare the nation of Israel to follow the way of the Lord that empowers *all human beings* to experience the salvation of God.

The desert the Baptist refers to, and the crooked ways that we must make straight, are not a physical desert or a physical path. The desert is the interior arid wasteland of the corrupted human conscience, filled with poisonous biting serpents, at times indifferent and often hostile, blind, and cruel when striking out against fellow human beings in desperate need. Often it is our response, or failure to respond, that determines whether those human beings live or die.

The hands up symbol in John's ikon of the Baptist means we choose to help them live; hands down means we let them die. It is far more of a challenge to attract the viewer's attention to the moral and spiritual symbolism embodied in the physical position of the Baptist's hands than to the physical image of a hair shirt or the barren natural environment of the desert.

The crooked ways to be straightened and the rough ways to be made smooth are the facile and slick mental and emotional stratagems we human beings rely on in our thinking. We use them to desensitize and deceive our own moral consciences and those of others. We use them in order not to feel guilty and to justify our self-preoccupations and moral indifference. We use them to make our actions, or inactions—which cause harm and even death to others—appear morally blameless, or even as deserving of praise and respect. People able to dominate others and compel them to submit to their will are instinctively revered and considered worthy of unquestioning respect.

The Baptist was not naïve. He was fully aware of the concentrated forces of fear, greed, resentment, lust, pride, arrogance, folly, and disregard for truth, lurking deep within human consciousness. These are the well springs of enormous levels of human violence throughout history and today, destroying families, races we deem inferior, entire cities and nations, all too often in the name of religion.

Today these fearsome forces threaten to lay waste our entire planet. Dark and corrupting energies lie like coiled poisonous serpents in human hearts and minds. At the slightest aggravation, they are ready with violence to rise up and strike out, with swift retaliatory vengeance, against any perceived threat or offense. This venomous snake in human hearts and minds is what led to the stoning and killing of the prophets in ancient Israel. It also led the religious authorities and people of their time to kill the Baptist and Jesus. We still see it in the violent assaults upon those who dare to speak as authentic moral prophets to "modern" societies today.

When crowds came out to hear him in the desert, the Baptist was aware he would face these destructive and corrupting forces, present in all human hearts and minds. He also knew that these destructive forces would inevitably recoil upon those falling prey to them. Both he and Jesus predicted that the growing resentment, moral corruption, arrogance, and desire for revenge dominating so many in Israel would lead to the annihilation of Jerusalem.

On his final journey to Jerusalem, resulting in his crucifixion, as he approached the city Jesus wept and cried out:

> *Would that even today you knew the things that made for peace!*
> But now they are hid from your eyes. For the days shall come upon you, when your enemies will cast up a bank about you, and hem you in on every side, and dash you to the ground, you and your children within you, and they will not leave one stone upon another in you; because you did not know the day of your visitation.
> *(Luke 20: 41-44)*

After the catastrophic failure of a major Jewish uprising against Rome, this prophesy came true in A.D. 70, resulting in the utter destruction of the city of Jerusalem and its Temple. Both were reduced to heaps of rubble and ashes. John recognized that the people's arrogant ethnic pride and sense of entitlement had made them feel foolishly secure as "God's chosen ones".

Conscious of what he faced, nonetheless he still preached his uncomfortable message to the crowds that came out to hear him in the desert:

> He said to the multitude who came out to be baptized by him
> "You brood of vipers! Who warned you to flee from the wrath to

come. Bear fruits that befit repentance, and do not begin to say to yourselves, 'we have Abraham as our father,' for I tell you, God is able from these stones to raise up children from Abraham. Even now the axe is laid to the root of the trees; every tree therefore that does not bear good fruit is cut down and thrown into the fire." And the multitude asked him, "What then shall we do?"

(Luke 3:7-10)

What then shall we do? is the critical focusing question. That so many asked this of him, even after his harsh words, speaks to a deep and authentic repentance, a genuine hunger for spiritual and moral renewal in the hearts of many. The Baptist's answer is equally relevant for discerning how God calls us to repent and to reset our priorities in the modern world today.

He who has two coats, let him share with him who has none; and he who has food, let him do likewise.

(Luke 3:10-11)

The Baptist warns the soldiers against extortion and using their weapons and superior force to shake people down, and tells them to be content with their wages. He also warns government officials against extortion, using their political powers to threaten people with harm if they don't do what serves their narrow self-interests.

What the Baptist demanded is very different from what was understood then, and still today, as explicitly religious: praying, reading sacred books, using the correct religious language, performing the prescribed external religious rites, dutifully obeying the religious authorities, etc. *The demands are moral; they specify the basic behaviors we should expect of any decent human being, of whatever religion or none.* His preaching of repentance, a true *metanoia*, is a call for active concern and compassion, a generous willingness to contribute from our life substance, and through our social and political actions to reach out and assist others, especially the most needy and vulnerable in our world.

Apart from these behaviors, our world will never become a more truth-seeking, kind, compassionate, merciful, and peaceful place. Any religion lacking these moral behaviors becomes selfish, cruel, corrupt, and filled with lies, a source of evil and violence rather than a source of truth, compassion, goodness, and peace. Any healthy religion must build upon these moral foundations. The New Testament does not, however, present the Baptist as making any demand that others follow him in his own austere religious and ascetic life in the desert.

There is another side to the story of the Baptist. In the mode of the Old Testament prophet Elijah, he is also a fiery, apocalyptic preacher. Elijah was a 9th century prophet who showed his divinely given power over the forces of evil by calling fire down from heaven and slaughtering the lying prophets who were leading Israel astray. (*I Kings 18:20-40*)

For two hundred years before the time of the Baptist and Jesus, and for about a hundred years after their deaths, Jewish authors produced a considerable body of apocalyptic writings, which have a different tone and content than in most of the Israelite prophets and in the New Testament Gospels. The Israelite prophets concentrated on issues of justice and mercy in the daily lives of their contemporaries. In contrast, the Apocalyptists focused on the wrath of God and violent speculations about "the final end of things and the destiny of the world in general." (*Oxford Dictionary of the Christian Church*, p. 67.)

These writings were largely an expression of the intense resentment of the Jewish people to the continual political domination of Israel for hundreds of years by foreign nations. The underlying assumption in these apocalyptic writings is that *God himself would finally rise up in wrath, destroy Israel's enemies, and set up God's kingdom on earth.*

The Baptist is a conflicted prophetic figure, caught between two radically different visions of how God will choose to deal with the problem of persistent and recalcitrant moral evil in our world. God could rise up in wrathful anger, destroying all the evil doers, and give full political power to his "chosen ones." Or God could choose a patient, kind, merciful, and long-suffering path, seeking not the death but rather the salvation of sinners, no matter how long, in human terms, this takes.

The Jewish Apocalyptists were convinced that the wrath of God would rise up and destroy all the evil doers. Second Isaiah's vision of a universal, loving, and merciful God, who desires salvation not just for the people of Israel but for all human beings, calls us to a different religious path.

I have come to see the Baptist as torn, deeply attracted to both of these very distinct religious visions. The Baptist's apocalyptic anger and rage strikes out at the crowds coming to him in the desert, addressing them all as "a brood of vipers," fleeing from "the wrath to come." Unless they bear good fruit, they "will be cut down and thrown into the fire." But we also see a breadth of mercy and compassion in his response to all those demonstrating genuine repentance when they ask: *What then must we do?* His answers reveal a deep longing that substantive mercy and compassion be shown to all:

> "He who has two coats, let him share with him who has none;
> and he who has food, let him do likewise."
>
> (*Luke 3:10-11*)

As we will see in the next meditation on the water baptism of Jesus by the Baptist, Jesus had a very different understanding of his mission as the Messiah than did John the Baptist. God anointed Jesus as the chosen one, whose task was not to restore Israel as an independent political power among the nations nor to seek any sort of worldly kingdom. He came to fulfill the divine will that "all human beings see the salvation of God." This required a very different focus, unfamiliar methods, and a new set of priorities.

When Jesus appeared before the judgment seat of Pilate, and would be condemned to death by crucifixion, Pilate said to him, "Are you the king of the Jews?" Jesus said:

> "My kingship is not of this world."
>
> (*John 18:33-36*)

> *Open, O Lord, our hearts and minds to true repentance,*
> *let us not take offense at this challenge,*
> *that we may also share with others*
> *the infinite power of your mercy and forgiveness.*
> *Through Christ our Lord.*

BAPTISM BY WATER

36" x 77"

1999

2

BAPTISM BY WATER

The Water Baptism is one of the largest panels in John Cobb's traveling ikon chapel. At three feet high and almost six and one-half feet wide, it depicts six different biblical figures, three from the Old Testament and three from the New.

The three Old Testament figures are Adam and Eve and the prophet Jonah. The message of the Book of the Prophet Jonah plays a critical role in understanding the spiritual message of the ikon. Few bible readers have discovered the depths of spiritual and moral richness contained in that remarkable prophetic work.

The New Testament figures are Jesus the Christ, John the Baptist, and a figure reminiscent of the account of Jesus' healing of the Gerasene demoniac in the Gospel of Mark.

Of all John's traveling chapel ikons, this is the most complex, from both an historical and a spiritual perspective.

This ikon, unlike the others, required the meditation to be divided into separate sections. Each is necessary to bring to voice the distinct witness of each of these diverse individuals and their different time periods. The importance of the different headings is similar to having different sections in a choir. Contrasting voices, ways of singing, and what is sung are fundamental to the harmony of the whole.

In this ikon we have a mighty chorus from across the centuries singing its praises of the ongoing and ever more inclusive movement forward of the eternal divine plan for the salvation of all flesh.

There are five sections:

1) Jesus and John the Baptist
2) Adam and Eve
3) The Book of the Prophet Jonah
4) The Gerasene Demoniac
5) *The Benedictus*

The physical landscape of the ikon is Hippie Hollow on Lake Travis, one of the largest lakes in Central Texas. An infamous nude swimming hole during the Hippie Era in the 1960s-70s, its past is recalled in the tiny figures of a naked Adam and Eve stepping down into the waters.

In his younger years, John was an active surfer on the Texas Gulf Coast near Corpus Christi and at favorite beaches in Mexico, Southern California, even Hawaii. He knew many of the major players. All of the individuals depicted in this ikon are his contemporaries. Everyone, except the fully clothed man in the foreground, is intimately involved with water—a surfer, a waterman, a plumber.

Most of Jesus' disciples were fishermen, also intimate with water. They experienced firsthand its power to generate life and also to take it. At the heart of the Baptist's preaching of a baptism of repentance are the themes of life and death. To repent is to die to an old way of life and be reborn to a new. And baptism, as understood in the New Testament, always involves death to a previous form of life, and rebirth in a new.

The ikon depicts a crowd of barefooted men responding to John the Baptist's urgent call to enter the waters of repentance, into a profound *metanoia* of both mind and heart. The men are cautiously stepping down a steep rocky shoreline into the waters below.

In the water, facing the crowd, urging them on, stands the Baptist, his arms upraised, his long hair sun-bleached, and his body burned brown from long exposure to intense sun. This depiction of the Baptist is very different than the gentle face of the homeless man in the previous ikon. A stridency, an urgency, a demanding character is revealed in this portrayal of the Baptist, consistent with his apocalyptic view of salvation.

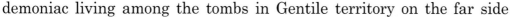

Only one figure, in the left foreground, is fully clothed. He appears curious, yet at the same time somehow detached from the scene. Reminiscent of the fearfully mad and terrifyingly strong Gerasene demoniac living among the tombs in Gentile territory on the far side of the sea of Galilee, he is a man Jesus would make sane and whole. In the bottom right corner, a man, who in real life had the name of the Old Testament prophet Jonah, resists the Baptist's call, his flesh twisting violently away from the waters of repentance.

In the nearer background in the center of the ikon, outlined against the gray stone cliffs, we see Adam already in the water. Eve's rests her hand on Adam's shoulder as she steps down into the water to join him. On the far shore is a vague outline of rising grey hills, and a yellow, orange-tinged sky, with light pouring down like rain from heaven above.

JESUS THE CHRIST AND JOHN THE BAPTIST

The two central figures in the ikon are Jesus the Christ and John the Baptist. Their eponyms are important. The Christ is the son of God and savior of the world. The Baptist is God's prophet from on high, preparing the way of the son of God. Among all the prophets, he alone pointed out the Lamb of redemption. John's baptism of repentance initiates a washing away of the moral barriers in human hearts and minds to the fulfillment of Jesus' teaching on the Kingdom of heaven. At first glance, the commanding figure of John standing in the water with upraised arms, confronting and urging the crowd to enter the waters, seems to be the central figure. But he isn't. Jesus is.

Jesus does not stand out. Nothing highlights his central importance or distinguishes him from the crowd, except perhaps his pale face, long black hair, and somewhat greater height. No external signs, no dove or divine voice comes down from heaven. Like all the rest, he is fully human, humbly preparing to enter side by side with them into a baptism of repentance and the forgiveness of sins.

In her *Catechism of the Catholic Church* (*CCC* 1223-1225), the Church explains her understanding of the figure of Christ in this scene, and Jesus' fulfillment of the Old Testament prophecies in submitting to John's baptism of water:

> All the Old Covenant prefigurations find their fulfilllment in Christ Jesus. He begins his public life after having himself baptized by John the Baptist in the Jordan...

> Our Lord voluntarily submitted himself to the baptism of St. John, intended for sinners, in order to "fulfill all righteousness."
> *(Matthew 3:15)*

> Jesus' gesture is a manifestation of his self-emptying. The Spirit who had hovered over the waters of the first creation descended then on the Christ as a prelude of the new creation, and the Father revealed Jesus as his "beloved Son."
> *(Matthew 3:16-17)*

> "In his Passover Christ opened to all the fountain of Baptism. He had already spoken of his Passion, which he was about to suffer in Jerusalem, as a 'Baptism' with which he had to be baptized."
> *(Mark 10:38)*

The blood and water that flowed from the pierced side of the crucified Jesus are types of Baptism and the Eucharist, the sacraments of new life.

The people of Israel celebrated the initial Passover in response to God's instructions to prepare for their exodus from slavery in Egypt. Each household was instructed to take a lamb, sacrifice it, "take some of the blood, and put it on the two doorposts and the lintel of the house in which they eat (the lamb)." (*Exodus 12:7*) That very night, when the power of death falls on the Egyptians and all their flocks and herds, death will *Pass Over* the Israelites and mark the beginning of their release from their bondage in Egypt.

This course of preparation would strengthen them for their forty-year journey through the wilderness to the Promised Land. But this first Passover and subsequent journey was a partial and imperfect prefiguring of the sacrifice which God himself would offer, one that would open the passageways from death to life, not just for some, but for all flesh.

To enter into the sacrifice of God's universal love, each of us must die from all forms of material and spiritual egoism and selfishness. Only in this way do we come to participate in the true nature of God's glory and Jesus' glory, and become members of a people *fit for the kingdom of heaven and able to find fulfillment and joy in it.*

The spiritual journey is the journey of unselfishing.

God's glory and Jesus' glory...

> has something to do with dying. But always, in (Jesus') many references to sacrifice, to abnegation, to dying, he is saying something very positive. It is not just that the grain of wheat falls into the earth and dies, and that's it. But this is for a purpose. Death is never its own end. Death is always a preface, a prelude, an avenue towards something better... God is glorified by every assent of the heart to whatever suffering God has planned as our part in the redemption of the world. Think of that. Always, when the heart assents to whatever sacrifice God asks, a larger picture opens out before us. The more God is glorified by the assent of the heart, the more do we see how God is asking us to glorify him further. This means that we die to self-

involvement, to entanglements, to what would make us remain alone with self, involved with self, entangled with self—a terrible state to be in. We want to lead lives of much dying so that much fruit can spring up. This is what it is to glorify God.

> (Mother Mary Francis, P.C.C.,
> *Magnificat*, Holy Week 2020,
> Vol. 22, No. 1, pp. 67-68)

In the world, we experience much anger and hostility among different individuals and groups, within the intimacy of the family, in our churches, at work, in politics, and among different religions. We experience it within ourselves. In the New Covenant, *Christ shed his blood for all*, and "abolished in his flesh the law of commandments and ordinances that he might create in himself one new humanity" in place of all tribal hostilities and religious warfare, reconciling all "to God in one body through the cross, thereby bringing the hostility to an end." (*Ephesians 2:11-22*)

The Good News of the New Covenant in Christ is the revelation of the full mystery of the Divine Will since before the creation of the world. Step by step God is making...

> "known to us in all wisdom and insight the mystery of his will,
> according to his purpose which he set forth in Christ as a plan
> for the fulness of time, to unite all things in him, things in
> heaven and things on earth."
> (*Ephesians 1:9-10*)

In the first creation, God willed into being all things visible and invisible. This is only the first step in a progressive process extending through the ages by which God enables "one new humanity." All human beings are called to participate in this ministry of reconciliation. Even before the creation of the world, God's eternal and unchanging purpose was the achievement of this celestial symphony, the harmony and reconciliation of all things.

God chooses not to accomplish this ultimate fulfillment alone, but requires our voluntary and free cooperation with the Divine Will. In God's ongoing dialogue with St. Catherine of Siena (1347-1380), medieval mystic, social reformer, and first female Doctor of the Church, he often reminds her:

I created you without your help, but I will not redeem you without your help.

(The Dialogue 226, 276, 330)

In Paul's letter to the *Colossians,* we encounter one of the strongest statements in Scripture of a central paradox of Christian teaching and its extraordinary elevation of the central importance of human freedom in the order of creation. This is the unfathomable decision of the omnipotent Creator, out of love for his creation, choosing to make himself dependent upon the choices of human beings to achieve the redemption of the cosmos: *I rejoice in my sufferings for your sake, and in my flesh I complete what is lacking in Christ's afflictions, for the sake of his body the Church.* (1:24)

In the lives and teaching of the Saints, this is a constant theme. Pope Francis emphasizes this same enduring truth today: "the building of the (kingdom of God) requires not only the grace of God but also the active willingness of humanity." (Sunday, July 26, 2020, *Angelus* commentary)

But why did God not create a world so perfect that no evil could exist in it? With infinite power God could always create something better. But with infinite wisdom and goodness God freely willed to create a world "in a state of journeying" towards its ultimate perfection. In God's plan this process of becoming involves the appearance of certain beings and the disappearance of others, the existence of the more perfect alongside the less perfect, both constructive and destructive forces of nature. With physical good there exists also physical evil as long as creation has not reached perfection."

(CCC 310)

Angels and human beings, as intelligent and free creatures, have to journey toward their ultimate destinies by their free choice and preferential love.

(CCC 311)

Jesus' initial hiddenness among the crowd coming to the Baptist is itself a manifestation of his essential "self-emptying" in service of others. This is the heart of his mission and its ultimate fulfillment in his sacrifice on the cross. He calls each of us to this same path, the only path leading to heaven and the victory over sin. Christ, the son of God, comes among humankind not as one to be served but as one who serves.

> Those healed by Jesus were freed not only from sickness, sin, or evil, but more especially from the potential self-centeredness of the suffering.
>
> (*Magnificat*, July 2020, p. 306)

As the son of God, Jesus also possesses the highest kingly authority. It does not come from human beings, or any established socio-political structure, whether religious or secular, but directly from God. John Cobb drew upon the classic figures of the Pharaohs in ancient Egyptian art, to depict the kingly and divine authority of Jesus. They were his models for presenting the mysterious figure of Jesus, not only as a servant figure submitting himself to others' needs, but as the Redeemer King, the Lamb of God, who lays down his life for others and triumphs over death by the power of his resurrection. His face radiates a calm, determined certitude and power.

The image does not rely on a physical crown or scepter and throne to convey this. Jesus is stripped to his black trunks, yet his face and posture reflect the ancient, ideal of an interior regal majesty and tranquility as he moves without hesitation into the waters of repentance. Already he looks beyond the Baptist, to his solitary forty-day fast and one-on-one combat with Satan in the desert, then to his choosing of the Apostles and his ministry of teaching and healing in Galilee. Only then comes the consummation in his final journey to Jersualem, his death on the cross, resurrection, and the sending of the Holy Spirit upon the church.

Crafted with great care, the ikon depicts the central, mysterious, and paradoxical Christian teaching of the humility of God in Jesus, God's self- revelation in our world, as *the Suffering Servant-King*. He is not a king who comes with sword and military might. Neither swords nor bullets nor any kind of physical force will achieve the Kingdom of God that Jesus preached, and the life prefiguring that Kingdom he empowers us to share. Acts of violence always disfigure the moral and spiritual beauty of the human soul created in the image and likeness of God. Violence cannot restore the soul's beauty.

Looking deeper, we discern the tangible differences distinguishing Jesus from all the other figures in the ikon, including the Baptist. The striking contrast between the face and posture of Jesus and that of the Baptist are deliberate. This Baptist is very different from the depiction in the previous ikon of a non-threatening, young homeless man. This John is strident, urgent, and demanding, an apocalyptic prophet in the manner of Elijah.

The calm and kingly dignity of Jesus, who comes not to be served but to serve, highlights the dramatic contrast between what the Baptist expected of the son of God, and how Jesus would in fact carry out his mission as God's chosen one. The Lamb of God takes away the sins of the world by his rejection of violence and his humble submission to death on a cross for all flesh.

At first, the crowds coming out to hear John preach in the desert focused all their attention on the Baptist. Many believed he might be God's chosen one, the long-expected Messiah, who comes to set God's people free. In the Gospel of St. John, the Baptist himself insists that people should turn their focus from him to Jesus. He states clearly that he is not the Messiah and that his role must diminish even as Jesus' increases.

The Baptist is the one who first refers to Jesus both as the son of God and as "the Lamb of God who takes away the sin of the world" (*John 1:24-37*). The Baptist confesses that God himself revealed Jesus' significance to him as he baptized him. The descent of the Holy Spirit upon Jesus and the voice of God affirming from heaven, "This is my beloved son with whom I am well pleased", revealed to the Baptist that Jesus was God's chosen one.

Of himself, he said,

> "I baptize you with water; but he who is mightier than I is coming, the thong of whose sandals I am not worthy to untie; he will baptize you with the Holy Spirit and with fire."
>
> (*Luke 3:16*)

By teaching the necessity of a moral and spiritual conversion of heart and mind to the universal mercy and compassion of God, the Baptist prepares the way in his water baptism of repentance. Only through this conversion can we enter with joy into God's kingdom. But only Jesus the Lamb of God can overcome the power of death in our world. Neither human beings nor nature as a whole can accomplish this victory over death. In this natural universe, death is the ruler. To use the metaphorical language of modern astrophysics, it is a world in which even stars eat stars, and nothing lasts forever. Only God, the all-transcending omnipotent Creator, has the power to free all of creation from the violence and death that rules the natural world.

If there is no omnipotent, saving, merciful and redemptive God, then any promise of eternal joy and peace extended upon all flesh across the ages is a delusion.

The Baptist anticipated that Jesus would reform the existing institutional structures and religious practices in Israel, restoring both religious purity and political autonomy to the nation of Israel. He recognized that this required an inner moral and spiritual purity in human hearts and minds.

But he also believed that the ultimate goal could be fulfilled only when Jesus exercised his powers as a political messiah and became Israel's new King and political ruler. He expected Jesus to be a fiery reformer, exercising his power as the chosen one of God in apocalyptic ways, bringing down the destructive wrath of God both on the forces of corruption within Israel and upon her external enemies.

Jesus rejected this path. Instead he insisted that his kingdom is not of this world and refused all forms of political coercion and violence. He allows himself to be subjected to death by crucifixion by the worldly power of Rome. He commanded his disciples to follow this same path, also bearing their crosses, and never returning evil for evil.

Except the Apostle John, all of the Apostles would experience a violent death at the hands of the enemies of the Christian faith. God did not guarantee his followers any form of political protection. God is our spiritual protector and guide, and will bring us to eternal joy. This does not mean he always protects us from suffering, imprisonment, or death in this world.

When John was in Herod's prison prior to his execution, his disciples kept him informed about what Jesus was doing. The Baptist began to wonder if Jesus really was the long-expected Messiah.

> And John, calling to him two of his disciples, sent them to the Lord saying, "Are you he who is to come, or shall we look for another?" … In that hour (Jesus) cured many of diseases and plagues and evil spirits, and on many that were blind he restored sight. And he answered them, "Go and tell John what you have seen and heard: the blind receive their sight, the lame walk, lepers are cleansed, and the deaf hear, the dead are raised up, the poor have good news preached to them. And blessed is he who takes no offense at me."
>
> *(Luke 7:19-23)*

In reaching out to the most needy and vulnerable in our world, Jesus does what the Baptist himself demanded in his preaching of repentance. He heals the sick, lame, blind, deaf, comforts the socially rejected, feeds the hungry, and even raises the dead. He ministers to those grieving the death of loved ones. He preaches good news to the poor. To all of them, he was a powerful sign of God's mercy and compassion.

The disappointment often conveyed in the Gospels was that, even after the experience of physical miracles of healing, few showed the kind of interior repentance that both John and Jesus sought. Those whose bodies were healed failed to manifest a new zeal for extending God's healing and mercy to the most needy among them. Instead, many took offense at both John's and Jesus' preaching of repentance. They went on with their lives just as selfish and indifferent to the needs of others as before. Any direct criticism of the immorality of their lives was received as an unbearable offense. The blessed who took no offense at him were those able to receive his moral criticism with open hearts and minds, repent, and reform their lives.

The Gospel of Luke provides a prime illustration. Jesus encounters ten lepers and he heals them all. But only one of the ten returns to give thanks. He was not even a member of the chosen people of God. He was a Samaritan, regarded by Jews as a despised foreigner and religious heretic.

Then said Jesus, "Were not ten cleansed? Where are the nine?

Was no one found to return and give praise to God except this foreigner?" And he said to him "Rise and go your way; for your faith has made you well."

(Luke 17:11-19)

Physical miracles alone do not open hearts to the spiritual reality of the kingdom of God. Jesus many times told people not to share this news of the external, physical miracles of healing because he did not want people coming to him seeking only physical external benefits. Only the inner miracle of a genuine repentance and the opening of hearts and minds to new priorities and new ways of living, unlocks the doors to the kingdom he preached. Jesus desired among his followers a positive embrace of the sufferings and sacrifices life inevitably places before us as important to our freely chosen participation in his own redemptive sacrifice and sufferings on the cross. This way of life can be successfully lived only with the steadfast help of the stout walking staff of the virtues of faith, hope, and love infused by divine grace.

We must learn how to love apart from receiving consolations and rewards.

Jesus non-violent approach to achieving the kingdom of God left the Baptist dismayed and confused in his prison cell. He believed that God's Kingdom could only come into being in apocalyptic, violent, this-worldly ways. He seemed unconvinced that the other-worldly, non-violent and non-political ways of Jesus could ever achieve it.

It is not surprising that Jesus says of John the Baptist:

"I tell you, among those born of women none is greater than John; yet he who is least in the kingdom of God is greater than he."

(Luke 7:29)

Jesus' criticism of John the Baptist in the Gospel of Matthew, a criticism that implicitly includes his predecessor the prophet Elijah, focuses precisely on the issue of violence.

"From the days of John the Baptist until now the Kingdom of Heaven has suffered violence and men of violence take it by force."

(Matthew 11:12)

Jesus turns his face away from this path and commands all his followers to do the same.

> "You have heard that it was said, 'an eye for an eye and a tooth for a tooth.' But I tell you, Do not resist one who is evil. But if any one strikes you on the right cheek, turn to him the other also; and if anyone would sue you and take your coat, let him have your cloak as well; and if anyone forces you to go one mile, go with him two miles. Give to him who begs from you, and do not refuse him who would borrow from you."
>
> *(Matthew 5:38-42)*

Heaven is *the only place where the joy of each can truly become the joy of all*. People fit for the Kingdom of Heaven are characterized by their hunger and thirst for this universally sharable joy. This is the true hunger and thirst for the righteousness spoken of by Jesus' in his beatitudes. (*Matthew 5:3-16; Luke 6:17, 20-23*) We must desire first of all to meet the needs of others more than our own.

The test of the authenticity of this desire is our persistence in loving even when we receive no consolations or rewards. If we do not have that resolve, then even if God himself were to set us down smack dab in the middle of heaven, we would take offense. We will still be angry at anyone not like us and still resentful towards everyone we believed had offended or injured us.

By our own personal choices we would find ourselves condemned to the eternal wretchedness of the unquenchable fires of perpetual anger, self-pity, and resentment. (Cf. C.S. Lewis' exploration in *The Great Divorce* of the fundamental nature of the choice between heaven and hell. In this creative tale of a bus ride transporting people from hell to heaven, the bus driver is Christ himself. Almost everyone from hell, after getting a taste of the reality of heaven, spits it out and chooses to return to hell.)

The moral and spiritual transformation the Baptist preached is not sufficient to overcome the rule of sin and death over this world. Freely chosen human participation is required in the ongoing journey of redemption. Our growing freedom and commitment to caring for others points to progress in this journey. But the actual triumph over the power of death, and the universal redemption of all things, past, present, and future, is only fulfilled by God in the new creation.

ADAM AND EVE

In comparison to the others, the physical figures of Adam and Eve are small, but their placement at the very center of the ikon is symbolic, representing the temporal and spatial universality of the redemptive power of the Lamb of God's sacrifice upon the cross.

As humanity's first parents, Adam and Eve are the biological source of the unity of the human family. This genetic oneness of all human beings dissolves any reputed superiority of one race over another. We all are members of the same family, each of us blood relations to all the others, all brothers and sisters. But Adam and Eve are also the initiating point for the betrayal, brokenness, and violence within the human family.

In the figurative language of the Book of Genesis, Adam and Eve, our first parents created in the image and likeness of God, were also the first human beings to sin, falling by their own choice "from God's friendship and grace." (CCC 391-392) Their sin is not reducible to a simple human rebellion against the absolute authority of God. The root of their sin "is an abuse of the freedom that God gives to created persons so that they are capable of loving him and loving one another." (CCC 387) The human spiritual capacities of freedom, love, knowledge, and creativity are the constitutive aspects of our human nature created in the image and likeness of God. Not a physical image, it is a spiritual one, equally present in women and men. The tragedy of sin is the unleashing of powerful and persistent negative and seductive forces within us, female and male, that rip apart faithful committed love, compassion, knowledge, truth, positive creativity, and forgiveness.

But no matter how great the anguish and destructive burdens of the past, it is fundamental Christian teaching that the mystery of God's creative power and redeeming love are infinitely greater than the mystery of the destructive powers of evil at work in our world.

In modern science, the arrow of time generally is understood as flowing only in one direction, toward the future, not reversible, unable to flow backward to transform the past. In the biblical teaching of the universal redemption of all flesh, no such temporal limitation exists. The omnipotent Creator makes available to every human being the passage from death to larger life. All that is required is the willingness to repent, accept forgiveness, and to turn from evil to good. The redemptive will of God transforms both space and time, reaching backward, embracing all human beings, including humanity's first parents, Adam and Eve.

The symbolism of Adam and Eve in the ikon, stepping unclothed into the waters of repentance, signifies that their nakedness is now no longer a source of shame. God restores them not just to their original innocence, but also to something now infinitely better.

The only truly unforgiveable sin in Christianity is our refusal to accept the infinite mercy and forgiveness of God. This is the foolish sinfulness and lack of trust manifested in believing our sins are more powerful than God's mercy. We reveal this disbelief in our refusal to extend forgiveness to others, including those who have sinned grievously against us. In denying them forgiveness, we are rejecting the universality of God's mercy; it is not God who rejects us. *God forgives us our sins against him, even as we forgive others their sins against us.* If we choose not to forgive, we have also chosen to reject God's forgiveness, not only of our own sins, but also of the sins of others.

Understanding the meaning of the petition in the Lord's prayer "forgive us our trespasses as we forgive those who trespass against us" is also fundamental to Jesus' great commandment that we love our neighbors as our selves. Just as we would not want forgiveness to be refused us, we should also not refuse it to others.

The central importance of Jesus' teaching upon this spiritual requirement in the Christian life is highlighted by St. Teresa of Avila, a 16th Century Spanish mystic, reformer, and founder of religious communities, and Doctor of the Church. In the midst of the terrible violence, moral and spiritual corruption in 16th Century Spain, she wrote to her religious sisters about the central religious importance of the love we show not just for God but also for others, including those who have sinned most grievously against us:

...how the Lord must esteem this love we have for one another!
Indeed, Jesus could have put other virtues first and said: forgive us,
Lord, because we do a great deal of penance or because we pray
very much and fast or because we have left all for You and love You
very much. He didn't say forgive us because we would give up our
lives for (God)... But he said only, "forgive us because we forgive."
(The Way of Perfection, p 180)

The ancient Eastern Orthodox iconography of the cross symbolizes this
traditional Christian belief in the infinite power of God's mercy to reach
back into time and redeem everything. At the base of eastern Christian
crosses we often see a skull, the skull of Adam. The Eastern Christian
tradition taught that Adam was buried in Palestine in the location called
in the New Testament Gethsemane, or Golgotha—*the place of the skull.*
The base of Jesus' cross is believed to have been set directly over Adam's
grave, physically and spiritually symbolizing that Adam and Eve, our
first parents, are also included in the Good News of Christ's joyous and
universal triumph over death through his sacrifice on the cross.

THE BOOK OF THE PROPHET JONAH

The Old Testament Book of Jonah contains a secret subject, not immediately apparent to the reader. I also did not understand this. When I first read
it, I was clueless. Only as I dug deeper and explored the wonderful wealth
of scholarship available today on these ancient biblical texts did I come to
understand the spiritual richness and contemporary relevance of its message.

The French Jesuit priest and psychiatrist, Fr. Arnold Uleyn, in his
work, *Is It I, Lord?*, most powerfully opened my eyes. His chapter on
Parables: an indirect method of bringing man to confess his sin fundamentally transformed not only my understanding of the Book of Jonah
but also of Jesus' use of parables in the Gospels. (*pp. 49-67*)

The Book of Jonah is one of the shortest books in the Bible, only about
three pages long. The human author is unknown, but scholars believe it
was written sometime between the 6th and the 3rd Century B.C.. It was
almost certainly written after Second Isaiah, who was the first of the
prophets clearly to refocus Israel's understanding of its divinely given
mission: God's eternal will is to bring the experience of salvation to all

flesh, not just to the nation of Israel.

There are many different kinds of literature in the Old Testament, not everything is history. The Book of the Prophet Jonah takes the form of a parable, a story intended to convey universal spiritual and moral truths, not historical facts. Its message is conveyed in a hidden and indirect way, similar to the ways that Jesus' delivered his most important teachings. He always spoke to the crowds through parables.

> "I will open my mouth in parables, I will announce what has lain hidden from the foundation of the world."
>
> *(Matthew 13:35)*

The principal subject of the Book of Jonah at first appears to be a rebellious prophet named Jonah and the astonishing response of the people of Nineveh. But the book is not what it seems. It was never intended to report historical facts, whether about a prophet swallowed by a big fish and then safely spit up on shore, or about an actual repentance of the entire city of Nineveh, including even its "many cattle." The unstated and secret subject is the chosen people of Israel. It is a book calling Israel to the same kind of moral and spiritual repentance that the prophet John the Baptist preached to Israel in the wilderness of Judea.

But Jonah, written nearly two and a half millennia ago, now also is for you and me. Each of us is included among its secret subjects. The challenge it presents is the same one it posed to ancient Israel:

Will we repent from our indifference and hardness of heart, our propensity to nourish grudges, and turn to the works of forgiveness, mercy, and justice?

The Book of the Prophet Jonah places a spiritual mirror before the face of every reader, whether ancient or modern. The challenge is whether we are open-hearted and mindful enough to grasp its application without taking offense.

In order to understand the spiritual message of the book, we must first understand Israel's historical experience with the city of Nineveh. Nineveh was the capital of Assyria, whose armies in 8th century B.C. had conquered the northern kingdom of Israel. Many of its religious and political leaders were killed or taken into exile and slavery. In the historical memory of

Israel, the great city of Nineveh became the epitome of savage aggression and power in the ancient world. Thus, when God commanded Jonah to go to Nineveh to preach repentance, he was sending the prophet to one of Israel's most violent, powerful, feared, and hated enemies.

This imaginative, humorous, and often ironical and satirical story begins with the word of the Lord coming to Jonah,

> "Arise, go to Nineveh, that great city, and cry against it; for
> their wickedness has come up before me."
>
> *(Jonah 1:1-2)*

But instead of going to Nineveh, Jonah flees from God's presence and took a ship heading in the opposite direction, to Tarshish. To grasp the central message of the book, we cannot be passive readers or hearers. We need to ask questions of the text and demand answers. We must be willing to dig deeper:

Why would someone chosen by the omnipotent God to be his prophet immediately disobey and do exactly the opposite of what God commanded? Was it a lack of courage, fear of going as God's messenger into the capital city of Israel's most feared, cruel and powerful enemy? What was the prophet's motive? *And what is the relevance of this to me?*

Not until the end of the story can the answers, and their application to each of us today, become clear.

The parable does not present us with simplistic, black-and-white caricatures of human beings, but rather with the universal and deeply human spiritual struggle between forces of good and evil. One force attracts and moves us forward beyond our narrow egotism to an ever-greater and more inclusive goodness, mercy and compassion. The other seduces and draws us backward, isolating us ever more within our own selfish egos and self-entanglement, making us less and less capable of forgiveness, fidelity, truth, mercy, and compassion. The Book of Jonah does not focus only on the sin of Jonah, or on our sins. It also draws attention to universal human capacities for mercy, compassion, courage, and repentance. It is also a story of the infinite mercy and compassion of God, who always accompanies each of us on this journey.

Jonah's theological message is that God alone is the true lover of humankind. God is alone ever faithful, never gives up on us. Over and over, he intervenes in countless mysterious ways, with great patience seeking to woo us back onto the right path.

The image of God universally present within human beings is the ultimate hidden source of the human attraction to an infinite, an ever greater, ever more inclusive, and eternal goodness.

In response to Jonah's waywardness, God sends a mighty storm upon the ship, threatening to sink it. When the pagan sailors discover Jonah is the cause of this disaster because of his disobedience to God, they ask him, "What then must we do so that the sea will quiet down?"

Jonah's unexpected response reveals the remarkable depth of his humanity. He is not lacking either in self-honesty or in the sacrificial courage manifest in genuine care for others, including those outside his own religious group. *He still bears within himself an active image of God.*

"Take me up and throw me into the sea; then the sea will quiet down for you; for I know it is because of me that this great tempest has come upon you." (*1:12*)

Then we also see a similar generosity and courage manifested in the pagan sailors, for they, too, are created in the image of God. Instead of wasting no time in tossing him overboard to save themselves, they struggle to save Jonah's life as well. They throw themselves into the effort to row the ship back to shore, but they could not prevail against the growing fierceness of the storm. At last, with regret and feelings of shame, they cast Jonah overboard, praying God will forgive them. At once the sea quiets down, and with reverent fear the pagan sailors offer sacrifices for forgiveness and vows of thanksgiving for God's saving mercy.

Right from the start we see the positive message of the universal capacity of compassion and courage at work in all the human players, both in God's rebellious prophet and in the pagan sailors.

Yet the irony is also clear. The pagan sailors, not members of God's chosen people, demonstrate a greater concern to obey God's will than his chosen prophet did. We see the same theme again in the pagan city of Nineveh's willingness to repent and obey God's will, even when God's chosen prophet would not.

But just as God showed his mercy on the pagan sailors, he also showers it upon his rebellious prophet. The Lord sends a great fish to swallow Jonah and rescue him from the raging sea. For three days and three nights, Jonah lives in the belly of the fish. Then God commands the great fish to spit him out upon the shore. Jonah gives thanks to God for his saving mercy.

A second time God speaks to Jonah:

> "Arise, go to Nineveh, that great city, and proclaim to it the message that I tell you." (*3:2*)

From the outside, Jonah appears repentant and willing to obey God's command, but inside his spirit remains unchanged, just as willful and disobedient as before. He exhibits no *metanoia*. He goes to the great city of Nineveh, so large it takes three days' journey to cover its breadth. He gives the briefest possible and a not very clear oracle of repentance to the Ninevites. It is only eight words in the English translation.

> "Yet forty days, and Nineveh shall be overthrown." (*3:4b*)

Miraculously, without requiring any further explanation, everyone in that vast city understands and repents. The king of Nineveh issues a proclamation for all of the city, its inhabitants, and all the living creatures.

> "Let neither man nor beast, herd nor flock, taste anything; let them not feed or drink water; but let man and beast be covered with sackcloth, and let them cry mightily to God; yea let everyone turn from his evil way and from the violence which is in his hands." (*3:7-8*)

Everyone, including the king and all the animals, cry out to God for mercy, and put on sackcloth. All fasted, "from the greatest of them to the least of them." (*3:5*)

> "When God saw what they did, how they turned from their evil way, God repented of the evil which he had said he would do to them, and he did not do it." (*3:10*)

So many incredible things spring forth from this astounding tale, raising all manner of questions and doubts in any thoughtful, engaged reader, whether among the ancient Israelites who first heard the story, or in a modern reader. For centuries, God sent prophets to the people of Israel, his chosen people, calling for repentance but very seldom with positive results. Often the response was simply to kill the prophet, the bearer of unpleasant demands that *they must change their way of life.*

Here we have a story of the Ninevites, the cruelest, most violent, and powerful of Israel's enemies. Yet all of them, from the mightiest to the least, and all the animals to boot, repent and turn from their terrible violence. And they do this after a single oracle of very few words by, of all things, a prophet from their enemy, Israel? The Ninevites repentance is profound; they admit their wrongdoing and express it through their outward actions of fasting, sackcloth, and ardent prayer.

They commit to the *metanoia* in which everyone is to *"turn from his evil way and from the violence which is in his hands."*

One must wonder how those in ancient Israel responded when they first heard this imaginative tale, filled with satire and humor, raising the deepest and most fundamental human questions. They knew quite well Assyria did not cease from the routine and cruel violence it inflicted on all the neighboring less powerful nations, until the yet mightier nation of Babylon defeated it. And just the thought of the cattle and all the other animals putting on sackcloth, fasting, and crying out to God for mercy, is pure comedy.

And yet the Book of Jonah was considered a serious, sacred, divine teaching from God himself, addressed to the nation of Israel. By expressing harsh criticisms of his chosen people, the teachings of the earlier Old Testament prophets had prepared Israel for a positive reception of this prophetic text. For over two millennia, the nation of Israel has revered Jonah, and through the continuing maelstrom of violence in the Near East, numerous devout Jewish people risked their lives to save this and all of the other sacred texts in the Old Testament. Preserving them was among their highest priorities.

These texts revealed in embarrassing and shameful, yet truthful, detail the corruptions and betrayals of the nation of Israel and its constant disobedience to the will of God. Although unfaithful to God in many ways, the people of Israel displayed a remarkable faithfulness in their conviction that it was worth risking one's life to preserve books like these with their powerful prophetic teachings. They were worth dying for.

Jonah's unexpected response, expressing his resentment and anger towards God, reveals why he "fled from God's presence." Usually a prophet is overjoyed when he preaches repentance and his audience actually repents. But in this case, when every Ninevite repented and, without one second of hesitancy, did exactly what God called them to do, Jonah was not at all happy about it.

> It displeased Jonah exceedingly, and he was angry. And he prayed to the Lord and said, "I pray thee Lord, is not this what I said when I was yet in my country? That is why I made haste to flee to Tarshish; for I knew that you are a gracious God and merciful, slow to anger, and abounding in steadfast love, and repents of evil. Therefore now, O Lord, take my life from me, I beseech you, for it is better for me to die than to live." (*4:1-3*)

Jonah is resentful towards God precisely because of his universal mercy and compassion. But still God does not give up on Jonah. God reaches out in patient dialogue to him yet again, challenging his priorities and foolish anger, and calling him to reconsider and repent.

> "Do you do well to be angry?"

> Then Jonah went out of the city and sat to the east of the city, and made a booth for himself there. He sat under it in the shade, till he should see what would become of the city. And the Lord God appointed a plant, and made it come up over Jonah, that it might be a shade over his head, to save him from his discomfort. So Jonah was exceedingly glad because of the plant. But when dawn came up the next day, God appointed a worm which attacked the plant, so that it withered. When the sun rose, God appointed a sultry east wind, and the sun beat upon the head of Jonah so that he was faint; and he asked that he might die, and said, "It is better for me to die than to live."

> But God said to Jonah, "Do you do well to be angry for the plant?

> And he said, "I do well to be angry, angry enough to die."

> And the Lord said, "You pity the plant for which you did not labor, nor did you make it grow, which came into being in a night, and perished in a night. And should not I pity Nineveh,

that great city, in which there are more than a hundred and twenty thousand persons who do not know their right hand from their left, and also much cattle?" (*4:4-11*)

God also does not give up on us. Jonah now becomes the *persona* representing not only Israel but also every reader of the Book of the Prophet Jonah. In this Book, with more than abundant patience, God reaches out to each of us. God is asking Jonah/Israel/us to reconsider the priorities by which we order our lives.

Are we also allowing "our little plant," that will in fact prove to be a very fragile and temporary protection and comfort in this world, to be our primary concern, even as we show no pity upon the vast numbers of those around us lacking the most basic necessities of life, whether they be friend or foe? Are we doing well when we do this? *Could we not, and should we not, be doing better?*

The Book of the Prophet Jonah now becomes a sacred spiritual mirror in which we see our own spiritual faces, if we dig deep enough and choose to open our minds and hearts. What blessings these biblical texts offer— to lift us up, move us forward, help us become kinder, more thoughtful, generous and forgiving people—if only we will listen, not take offense, and repent! Then, perhaps, we could even change our way of life.

THE GERASENE DEMONIAC

The fully clothed figure depicted in the foreground of the ikon on the left is a person discovered residing within a cave in the seawall carved out by the waves in Galveston. He lived a desperate life and slept often in a nearby graveyard on 61st Street. His anger and revulsion drove him to yell at all the cars. His leg was broken and had healed utterly misaligned, a visage of wild suffering to the passersby.

For those who know their New Testament, this situation recalls the account of Jesus' healing of the Gerasene demoniac in the Gospel of Mark (*5:1-20*). This was a man who lived among the tombs in the non-Jewish territory on "the other shore" of the Sea of Galilee. He is described as seeing Jesus "from afar" and running up "to worship him" in great fear and torment. He was a man...

"...with an unclean spirit, who lived among the tombs; and no one could bind him any more, even with a chain; for he had often been bound with fetters and chains but the chains he wrenched apart, and the fetters he broke in pieces; and no one had the strength to subdue him. Night and day among the tombs and on the mountains he was always crying out, and bruising himself with stones."
(Mark 5:1-5)

When Jesus asked him, "What is your name?", he replied, "My name is legion for we are many." (*5:9*) Jesus healed him, driving out the demons into a herd of swine, who then rushed down a steep bank into the sea and drowned. When the local townspeople heard of the healing of this man who had so terrified them, "they came to Jesus and saw the demoniac sitting there, clothed and in his right mind... and they were afraid... they began to beg Jesus to depart from their neighborhood." As Jesus was leaving, the man who had been healed "begged him that he might be with him. But (Jesus) refused and said to him,

"Go home to your family and friends, and tell them how much the Lord has done for you."

For all the advances in modern medicine, so many in our world today are still uncured, often living in the streets and very heart of our modern cities. These individuals suffer afflictions and torments in much the same ways as the Gerasene demoniac in ancient Palestine and the angry, possessed man in the modern city of Galveston that John depicts in this ikon.

John felt he deserved, most of all, to be near that calm expression and healing power of the vital, resolute, and kingly youth dressed in black shorts.

THE BENEDICTUS
The Canticle of Zecharia (*Luke 1:68-79*)

This biblical Canticle receives its name from the opening word *Benedictus*, meaning "Blessed" in the Latin translation of the original Greek. For centuries worshipers have prayed and often sung it in the daily morning prayers of the Church, following the appointed Psalms and biblical reading.

The division below into six stanzas is how the Canticle is structured for use in church liturgies. In much the same way as John's ikon of the Water Baptism, it highlights the contrasting voices and the different content of God's message in various periods of salvation history. The themes in the individual stanzas are constantly surging back and forth between past, present, and into a radically new future.

An important focus is on the fundamental continuities of God's faithfulness to his people in the past. But the ultimate fulfillment of God's chosen mission for Israel cannot be achieved by simply returning to the past. God's mission is larger and more inclusive than most of his chosen people have ever been able or willing to understand.

The most important message in the *Benedictus* is "that God's grace and favor is now to come to humanity in a new form..." (*Fitzmeyer 318*) The combined effect of the six different stanzas is to promote a living sense of the dynamic unity of the whole of salvation history as it moves forward step by step "in a state of journeying" toward its ultimate perfection. This perfection is only achieved in the "salvation of all flesh."

We best understand the radical newness of the New Covenant proclaimed in the *Benedictus* only when we are also able to comprehend it as a logical outgrowth of the Old. This process is a manifestation of God's patient leading of humankind, stage by stage through the centuries, to an ultimate perfection, spreading out in ever-wider circles. Already in Stanza 1, we see the shift from the Old to the New as we move from the first two verses to the final two verses. But the ultimate statement of what will be radically new comes to its fullest summary expression only in Stanzas 4 and 6. The role of John the Baptist as the key transitional figure between the Old and the New is celebrated in Stanza 5.

The challenge to the reader is that so much of this is only implicit and indirectly stated. This presents a challenge to our understanding very like the task of understanding Jesus' indirect teaching through parables. But to those who are familiar with the context of the texts and the relevant Old Testament history, and are hungry for a deeper discernment, the *Benedictus* opens new doors to a radical and fresh understanding of salvation history. It also offers a new insight into the nature of the path God calls all human beings to walk.

While these paths are prefigured in the Old Testament, the nature of the path, the methods, and the ultimate goal come to a much fuller and more exact expression in the New.

Jesus' submission to his water baptism is the critical moment.

Stanza 1
Blessed be the Lord, the God of Israel;
He has come to his people and set them free.
He has raised up for us a mighty savior,
Born of the house of his servant David.

Stanza 2
Through his holy prophets he promised of old
That he would save us from our enemies,
From the hands of all who hate us.

Stanza 3
He promised to show mercy to our fathers
And to remember his holy covenant.

Stanza 4
This was the oath he swore to our Father Abraham:
To set us free from the hands of our enemies,
Free to worship him without fear,
Holy and righteous in his sight
All the days of our life.

Stanza 5
You my child shall be called the prophet
Of the Most High;
For you will go before the Lord to prepare his way,
To give his people knowledge of salvation
By the forgiveness of their sins.

Stanza 6
In the tender compassion of our God
The dawn from on high shall break upon us,

To shine on those who dwell in darkness and the shadow of death,
And to guide our feet into the way of peace.

Filled with the Holy Spirit, Zecharia prophesies and sings this song of praise exactly eight days after John the Baptist's birth. A joyful celebration of family and neighbors takes place in his and Elizabeth's home in the hill country not far from Jerusalem. The gathering is for the purpose of the child's circumcision and naming. Choosing this specific day manifests Zecharia's and Elizabeth's obedience to the command given Abraham by God that a male child is to be circumcised on the eighth day after his birth. (*Genesis 17:12*) The emphasis on John's descent from priestly stock emphasizes his rootedness in the ancient traditions of Israel. But his ultimate role is to be the key transitional figure, making straight the way for God's New Covenant.

In the New Covenant, God will not write his law on tablets of stone or papyrus manuscripts, but on human hearts. (*Jeremiah 31:33-34*) As the spirit of the prophet Jeremiah foretold with great clarity, the radical demands of the New Covenant means it is no longer to be grounded in externals, but written interiorly, universally upon hearts and minds of human beings. As the initial Jewish-Christian community in Jerusalem, headed by the Apostles, continued to develop their faith in and under-standing of the New Covenant, many things in the Old Covenant once considered indispensable will be set aside: circumcision, the dietary code, the Temple services and its bloody animal sacrifices, and even the impor-tance of regaining political and military control over "the promised land". This did not happen without considerable conflict. (Cf. *Galatians 2:1-10, Acts 15:1-36*)

All of this was necessary to achieve what came to be understood as God's eternal will and mission for the true Israel: enabling the experience of salvation for all people, of every nation and tongue and time, to the ends of the earth.

Zecharia and Elizabeth are an elderly and childless couple. For years Elizabeth had borne great sorrow and a sense of shame about her barrenness as the wife of a Jerusalem priest, never able to bear him a child. And now, with the couple well beyond the age of childbearing, God blesses them with a son who will be the Prophet of the Most High.

Miraculous interventions mark all the circumstances surrounding the upcoming birth. The angel Gabriel first announces this coming birth to Zecharia in the Jerusalem Temple while he serves at the altar of incense. Because of his disbelief at the good news, Gabriel strikes Zecharia dumb. Now, eight days after the birth of his child, his tongue is loosed and he breaks into joyous song.

All these miraculous events manifest this as the work of God. And everyone wondered, saying:

> "What then will this child be? For the hand of the Lord was with him."
>
> *(Luke 1:66)*

This canticle of six stanzas provides a succinct summary in a song of praise of God's faithfulness throughout the history of salvation, beginning with God's covenant with Abraham and brought to fulfillment in Christ, God's word incarnate, the Dawn from on High, in Stanza 6.

Stanza 1

The opening two verses praise the fidelity of the God of Israel to his chosen people. God first calls them through his covenant with Abraham. Then whenever they fall into slavery, he frees Abraham's descendants time and again. God's steadfast faithfulness is manifest in his continual reaching out, despite his chosen people's constant obstinancy and disobedience to his will.

Israel has experienced three major episodes of exile and captivity in foreign lands. The first took place in Egypt, before they gained possession of the Promised Land. The other two periods occurred after disastrous defeats at the hands of foreign powers: the Assyrian Exile in the 8th century B.C., and then the Babylonian Exile in the 6th century B.C. In both cases, God performed miracles and freed his people from their captivity, bringing them back to the Promised Land.

No historical record exists of any other people in the ancient near East suffering this kind of national devastation and exile, and then returning to their homeland, two generations later, with their culture and religious traditions still intact.

Any devout Jew who knows Old Testament history would recognize the implicit reference in the *Benedictus* to the God of Israel's saving actions at the time of the Exodus from Egypt and the Assyrian and Babylonian exiles.

The rapid movement within the *Benedictus* from past to present, and then into a radical new future, is manifest already in the first stanza. The opening two lines focus on God's fidelity in the past through the covenant with Abraham. Then, in the last two lines, the Canticle shifts from the Old to the New. The object of focus is now Jesus the Christ, the mighty savior, born of the house of David, and the foundation stone of the New Covenant.

The radically new is what modern biblical scholarship refers to today as "the Christ event." It manifests God's power and might in ways radically different than in the Old Testament account of Israel's Exodus from Egypt or in the times of the Assyrian or Babylonian exiles. In the New Covenant, we encounter not just a celebration of the traditional belief in God's omnipotence. We discover an astonishing and unanticipated revelation of the new way the Creator of all things now chooses to reveal his power.

We meet a God who is humble, willing to empty himself of his own divinity in order to reveal the inexpressible depth of his passionate love for all that he has created. God is now revealed as *Immanuel*, God intimately with us, in our very flesh and bones, on our journey, fully sharing in all our human joys and sorrows.

Fr. Richard Vera, Director of Formation at St. Joseph's Seminary in New York, beautifully expresses this radical new revelation of the nature of God:

> The first characteristic we tend to ascribe to God is power. Certainly God is powerful; but he can reveal himself to us without manifesting his power: as a baby in a manger or a man suffering on a cross.

> St. John tells us that God is Love. Thus, God can never reveal Himself without love because love is Who God Is. Only love could bring God to the manger, or to the cross...

... (God's) humility towards us is a staggering revelation of his unfathomable love for us.

(2020 July *Magnificat*, p. 340)

Stanza 2

The second stanza returns to the Old Testament history in which the New Testament is grounded. It celebrates God's fidelity to his original covenant with Abraham recorded in *Genesis*, guiding him and his kindred from their native land into the Promised Land and making of his descendants a great nation. But God's original covenant with Abraham will not reach its fulfilment until the original blessings promised Abraham and his descendants are extended to *all the families of the earth. (Genesis 12:1-3)*

Stanza 3

The third stanza again emphasizes God's faithfulness in the past. Ever faithful, he manifests the mercy he promised to Abraham and his descendants in his original covenant. He rescued his people from the Egyptians, the Assyrians and the Babylonians. But because of the many victories of their enemies over them, many in Israel doubted the faithfulness of God to his covenant. They suspected the gods of the neighboring nations were, in fact, mightier than the God of Israel. The goal of this brief stanza is to strengthen confidence in God's faithfulness, with reminders of the multitude of ways God had rescued them in the past and set them free.

Stanza 4

In the fourth stanza of the *Benedictus*, the radical new understanding of the nature and will of God breaks through. God's chosen people must be willing to see the ultimate meaning of God's oath to Abraham in an unfamiliar way, a way very different from how ancient tradition expressed it in Israel. The emphasis now is no longer on the physical possession of the Promised Land, nor upon the external sign of circumcision, which marks the flesh but is unable to generate a universally merciful and compassionate heart. *Only opening minds and hearts in an authentic repentance to God's universal love and mercy keeps us on this path.*

Israel was obsessed with regaining political and military dominion over its enemies. What freedom from its enemies meant to Israel was possessing an overwhelming physical power bestowed by the omnipotent God. This required all the brutal physical force necessary to conquer, subjugate and take revenge for all the harms their enemies had inflicted upon Israel. Only this, they believed, could assure Israel's preeminent greatness and glory as God's chosen people among the nations of the earth.

We have already examined this obsession at work in the mind and heart of Jonah as the *persona* of Israel, whose burning resentment could only find satisfaction in the complete and utter destruction of Nineveh. As we have already seen in the prophet Second Isaiah during the Babylonian Exile, God had a much greater and more inclusive mission for Israel. It was not to be by "a cosmic stroke of the power of (the God of Israel)" to move Israel into the throne of World Empire currently occupied by Babylon. (John L. McKenzie, *Anchor Bible*, Second Isaiah, LVI) God's supreme mission for his chosen people was to make them "a light to the nations," his chosen instrument for bringing salvation to all flesh, not death and destruction.

The only way ultimately to achieve this was for God to free the true Israel from the violent, deadly and cruel competition among the nations for dominance of physical territory.

God desired to bestow upon Israel freedom from the hands of its enemies, but the freedom intended was of a very different nature than Israel desired, as well as many who call themselves "Christians" today. It was freedom from the lust for domination and revenge that has always been the enemy of peace and thus always humankind's greatest enemy. In the last three verses of Stanza 4 of the *Benedictus* we are informed about what this new kind of freedom will look like.

It is the courageous freedom to worship God without fear, holy and righteous in God's sight all the days of our lives, everywhere and whatever the external circumstance.

True and fundamental "holiness and righteousness" require a life characterized by humility, open-hearted truth-seeking, and living with kindness, forgiveness, mercy, and compassion, especially for the most needy. Freedom to live in this way is what God most desires to empower in humanity. This kind of living is the true worship of God, but it is only possible if we say "yes" to the gift. Only in this way does the salvation of all flesh become possible. This is the freedom offered by God in the New Covenant proclaimed by the *Benedictus*. It is a holiness and righteousness extending God's universal love and mercy to all, in every place and circumstance.

We have seen the importance of the universalist witness in Second Isaiah in John the Baptist's preaching of repentance in the barren deserts of Judea. The testimony of this prophet manifests a new and developing understanding of God's ultimate will for humankind, though the hostility to it, both in the ancient and in our modern world, was and remains fierce. This new understanding generates a new focus and receives stronger and clearer expression in the New Covenant proclaimed in the New Testament, five hundred years after its initial prefiguring by the prophet in exile in Babylon.

The historical period within which the writings of Second Isaiah emerged begins with the complete and utter destruction of Jerusalem and its holy Temple by the Babylonians under Nebuchadnezzar in 587 B.C.. Thousands were taken into exile into Babylon. Both the literary and archeological evidence clearly demonstrate that the defeat was a shattering disaster. "Not only Jerusalem but most of the fortified cities were left in ruins and some of the cities were deserted for generations after the war." (McKenzie, Introduction, p. XXIV)

Only within the exile community did the living traditions of Israel and new developments in the understanding of God's ultimate purposes for humankind expand. In 559 B.C., Cyrus II succeeded to the throne of Persia. In the writings of Second Isaiah, Cyrus emerged as a new kind of messianic figure in the history of Israel. The rising to prominence in Second Isaiah's glorification of the pagan king of the pagan nation of Persia was regarded as scandalous to many in the exile community. Yet the prophet continued vigorously to proclaim it was God's will that, through the hands of Cyrus, King of the Persians, Israel would be redeemed from its captivity in Babylon and restored to Jerusalem.

It was now two generations since the destruction of Jerusalem. The city remained uninhabited and in utter ruins. No one in the exile community had any living experience or memory of Jerusalem. The idea that God would soon restore them to their physical homeland through the pagan king of Persia was dismissed by most in the exile community as preposterous.

Then Persia under Cyrus conquered Babylon and "treated the defeated king and the city benevolently... " (McKenzie, Introduction, p. XXIX) And in 539 B.C., he issued a decree permitting the resettlement of a Jewish community in Palestine and the restoration (of the Jerusalem Temple and its worship)." The glowing terms in which Second Isaiah speaks of Cyrus attest to his belief that a new kind of conqueror had appeared in the world.

> In a certain way Cyrus lent himself to the conception of a "messianic" figure in the broad sense of the term, a savior-hero sent by (God) at a time when the people of (God) could not hope for a savior figure drawn from themselves. The Israelite prophet could see in a man of such stature one in whom the spirit of (God) had fallen. The empire of Cyrus foreshadowed the reign of (God) over all the nations. (McKenzie, Introduction, pp. XXX)

However, the essential spiritual movement from what is less to what is more important, from the exterior to the interior, and from the transitory to the eternal does not come to complete expression in Second Isaiah. He remains focused on Israel's return to the promised land in Palestine. As we have seen, Israel's obsession with regaining control of the promised land in Palestine continues to foster narrow nationalist perspectives that always puts their own nation first and generates not just spiritual opposition but fierce hostility to God's will for the salvation of all.

Thus the hostility of the prophet "Jonah" to God's universal love and mercy, rejecting the ways of peace and preferring death to life, continues its festering, dark and destructive presence in deeply unrepentant "religious" individuals and communities, Christian and non-Christian, around the world still today.

The Jesuit priest, Fr. John L. McKenzie, an internationally recognized Old Testament scholar, explicitly addresses this in his Anchor Bible commentary on Second Isaiah. He writes...

> The promises to Zion now reach a point of magnificence that goes beyond any mere historical reality of the restoration of Jerusalem. The point of the imagery is that (God) is founding a

lasting city, one that will not again suffer the fate of the Jerusalem of the monarchy. What would the prophet have said if he were told that the restored Jerusalem would be laid in ruins in 70 A.D. by the legions of Titus? But the vision of the prophet here approaches the eschatological: the lasting city of (God's) good pleasure is not a material reality of walls and building located at a definite point of longitude and latitude; it is the community of the redeemed. Of all those who are "instructed of God" and are "established in righteousness." Such a community will outlast any material structure in which it happens to be incorporated at a given moment of history. This is the indestructible Jerusalem which no enemy can harm. The righteous of (God) is a foundation stronger than any material foundation, proof against any human effort, even the effort of those who dwell in Jerusalem to corrupt it. (John L. McKenzie, p. 140)

The people of Israel began to experience this new spiritual freedom while in exile in Babylon. During that exile, synagogue worship, separate from the Temple, and a type of worship that could be made available everywhere, took root and spread. There are no complaints in Second Isaiah during the exile about God's chosen people becoming corrupt, unjust, and oppressors of the poor. But the problem reemerges in Third Isaiah, when the people returned to the Promised Land to rebuild the Temple and regain control over their physical territory. Once again the oppression of the poor by the wealthy and powerful becomes a central concern for the prophet.

A radical distinction was then drawn between the true Israel, consisting for the most part of the poor and oppressed, and the false Israel, consisting of the wealthy and governing classes. This was a constant distinction maintained in the post-exilic prophets. (Cf. the scathing criticism of animal sacrifices in the Temple worship and cereal offerings in *Isaiah 66:1-4*) The central importance in Jesus' teaching on the poor and our outreach to them is clear in his teaching on the final judgment in Matthew 25:31-46. It is further highlighted in the Beatitudes, his teachings on the new age he comes to introduce that will reach fulfillment only in the Kingdom of Heaven. (*Matthew 5: 1-15* and *Luke 6:17, 20-23*).

The freedom to worship God free from the fear of our enemies "holy and righteous in his sight" achieves its ultimate witness and fulfillment in Christ's sacrifice on the cross. But all those who call themselves his disciples are also called to pick up their cross and follow him. The freedom to which God calls us is no longer the empowerment envisioned in the Old Testament to pick up swords and slaughter enemies. The call and witness in the New Covenant, and the empowerment Christ offers, whatever one's location and physical circumstances in life, is to walk without violence the way of faith and love even when living in the midst of sin, evil and violence. (*Fr. Arseny, A Great Cloud of Witnesses*, p. 224.)

Father Arseny gave steadfast witness to this manner of life throughout his nineteen-years of brutal labor and imprisonment in Stalin's Gulag Archipelago. His crime was openly professing and teaching the Christian faith. Throughout those savage and brutal years he lived in God in prayer, bearing the burdens of others, and doing good not for his own benefit but for theirs. And he is not alone. There are countless others among the saints, known and unknown, who have given the same witness in violent and corrupt times throughout the centuries. In his story about life in these camps, Fr. Arseny himself speaks of many others in the camps who also lived this authentic life of faith. (Cf. *Fr. Arseny, 1893-1973*, pp. 40-48) His life is a powerful witness to the truth of his words which we have placed in the frontispiece of this volume:

> *The most magnificent and sacred treasure we shall encounter*
> *in this world is the human soul filled with faith, love and*
> *kindness, no matter the external circumstances of his or her life.*

When the spiritual virtues of justice, kindness, and mercy are missing, every form of "religion" becomes cruel, debased, and corrupted by human lusts for physical pleasure, dominance, and material possessions. From the preaching and witness of the Old Testament prophets and from John the Baptist's preaching of a baptism of repentance, we have seen what authentic holiness and righteousness look like. This understanding of "holiness and righteousness" continues to be vehemently rejected by many today who identify themselves as "religious". And the most angry and violent rejection manifests itself today, as in the past, among those who most loudly insist that they alone represent the cause of "true religion."

Stanza 5

Zacharia's friends and family raise a fundamental question about John:

"What then will this child be?" For the hand of the Lord was with him.

(*Luke 1:66*)

The answer lies in Stanza 5. He is "the prophet of the most High," preparing the way of the Lord, making straight the crooked paths in the desert of our corrupted consciences. If we do not practice humility, patience, self-control, chastity, mercy, compassion, and kindness, we will find no path leading to the Lord. The task of the Baptist is to prepare our hearts and minds for this kind of repentance, so that we can walk the paths of the all-inclusive and universal mercy and kindness to which Jesus is calling each of us.

But this kind of repentance is only a necessary beginning, the first step in a long and arduous journey. As we walk, we will encounter much suffering and many things which human beings are powerless to overcome. This includes the power of death which ultimately triumphs over every natural thing in the universe.

It is spiritually helpful daily to be mindful of the truth stated in the New Testament book of Hebrews:

"Here we have no lasting city, but we seek the city which is to come." (*13:14*)

Only Jesus, the Son and Lamb of God, gives us victory over the power of death and darkness in our world, and guides our feet into the way of eternal peace.

Stanza 6

In the tender compassion of our God
The dawn from on high shall break upon us,
To shine on those who dwell in darkness and the shadow of death,
And to guide our feet into the way of peace.

The Christ, not the Baptist, is "the tender compassion of our God, the dawn from on high". This is the Light that will break upon all those "dwelling in darkness and the shadow of death and guiding their feet into the way of peace." Only as we open our minds and hearts to this light of God's mercy, compassion, and peace in the midst of the griefs and sorrows of this world can we discover and remain on paths to the peace that shall not pass away.

The witnesses across the centuries to the transforming power of this supernatural, uncreated light "from on high" are countless. The authenticity of the experience does not lie in its immediate emotional intensity, which can be fleeting. Rather it lies in the enduring moral transformation and commitment for the rest of our lives to sharing God's mercy and compassion for the neediest among us. In the Introduction we wrote at some length on the modern medical research into the powerful transforming experience of "the light from on high" in near death experiences (NDEs).

John Newton, author of *Amazing Grace*, is among that great crowd of witnesses to the depth and steadfastness to the new way of living that flows from this experience of "the Light from on High." *Amazing Grace* is the most widely known and often sung Christian hymn today. But few who sing it, even with emotional intensity, possess any understanding of the depth of moral transformation and steadfast moral commitments its author manifested.

Infamous for his debauchery and cruelty, John Newton was a captain of slave ships. On March 21, 1748, in the midst of the Atlantic, a terrifying storm struck his ship, which seemed certain to take it down. His years of experience at sea left him with no doubt that the survival of his ship and all on board was a miracle of God's grace and mercy. Though not medically classified as a Near Death Experience, it was clearly an experience of the Light of Grace from on High. That miracle led him to repent from the inhumanity and depravity that characterized his former life.

He became a minister of the Gospel and a radical social activist. For the remainder of his life, he labored steadfastly to abolish the institution of slavery and all its cruelties. In this transformation of how he lived, John Newton provided a powerful witness to the positive fruits of authentic repentance demanded by the Baptist's preaching in the deserts of Judea two millennia ago. But he is only one of countless numbers across the ages, bearing witness to the enduring moral and transformative power of this Light.

Later he wrote about that day in 1748 when his slave ship tossed in the stormy Atlantic with death staring him and his sailors in the face. He used words reminiscent of the *Benedictus* to express his gratitude for the tender mercy of God descending upon him "from on high" and saving him from certain death:

> *On that day the Lord sent from on high and delivered me out of deep waters.*

As an old man, almost sixty years later, he wrote in his dairy on March 21, 1805:

> *Not well able to write; but I endeavor to observe the return of this day with humiliation, prayer, and praise.*

The hymn *Amazing Grace* has an especial importance to John Cobb and me. We use it in an outreach ministry to a Special Nursing Care facility in east Austin for a low-income population. For many years we have offered a weekly Catholic communion service there with another close friend, Jaime Mewis. *Amazing Grace* is the hymn the community demands, both at the opening and the closing, as they gather for this communion service. The informed prayers for one another's needs, joys, and sorrows from that community of faith and also for the staff caring for them, is always a spiritual inspiration for us for the remainder of the week.

Many at the point of dying have encountered this light that lifts one up and guides one to heaven. Some in our modern and scientific world dismiss such experiences as momentary hallucinations generated by the biochemical and neurological chaos of dying. In the introduction, I discuss the careful empirical research of medically trained professionals into the Near Death Experience (NDE's). Neither they nor I see these studies as scientific proof of another and very different reality awaiting us after death when our souls separate from our bodies. Sometimes we are required to walk by faith, not by sight. What they do document is the indisputably positive and enduring impact "the Light from on High" has on people's lives.

Those of us who have experienced it know firsthand the power of that transforming Light. Though perhaps never experienced again with that same intensity, it continues to guide us for the remainder of our lives on the steadfast path to an ever-greater goodness. It scarcely seems apt to describe as a 'momentary hallucination' what has the demonstrated power to transform one's life and to redirect it for a lifetime of genuine care and service to others. Whatever its source, its power to bring about the powerful moral transformation, the *metanoia* John the Baptist called for in his preaching of repentance, is indisputable.

For most of us who have experienced it, a more apt way of speaking about it is found in the Anglican *Book of Common Prayer's* burial service. This is Light from on High that has not only transformed us in this life, but will also guide and accompany us at the end of our lives through *the gates of larger life.* Or in the words of the ancient song of the *Benedictus,* it is *the Light from on High that breaks upon those dwelling in darkness and in the shadow of death, and to guide their feet into the way of peace.*

It is also the light symbolized in John's ikon of Baptism by Water, above the vague outline of the rising grey hills on the far side of the lake. It is the Light from on High, penetrating a yellow, orange-tinged sky, and pouring down like rain from heaven above.

Lord, you have renewed the face of the earth.
Your Church throughout the world sings you a new song,
Announcing your wonders to all.
Through a virgin, you have brought forth a new birth in our world;
Through your miracles new power;
Through your suffering, a new patience;
In your resurrection, a new hope,
And in your ascension a new majesty.

(*Christian Prayer: Liturgy of the Hours*, Psalm Prayer, 871)

BAPTISM BY FIRE
82" x 34"
2010

3

BAPTISM BY FIRE

In the Eastern Orthodox tradition, ikons are "written," not painted. They are spiritually understood as "the pictorial or symbolical representation of Christian ideas, persons, and history." They are meditative works flowing from the prayer and disciplined spiritual life of the iconographer. The true iconographer "writes" in paint with mind and heart open to the presence of Christ, the interior teacher.

At almost seven feet across and three feet high, this is the largest and most intricately detailed natural landscape of the ikons, three years in the crafting.

The work began as a large and intricately detailed landscape. It then gradually morphed into what became a symbolic representation of the liturgical themes of Easter and Pentecost. This translation of what initially appears a purely natural setting, into an incarnation in egg tempera and gold leaf of the ancient and eternal truths of the Gospels is the hallmark of Cobb's work as an iconographer.

The physical scene is a composite of settings drawn from the rugged Texas Hill Country and an abandoned rock quarry in Austin. The quarry is on the grounds of the Highland Park Elementary School that John attended from the 1st to the 6th grade. Scenes from the Texas Hill Country provide the backdrop. Everywhere we see detailed depictions of the rocky formations and ledges characteristic of the countryside, and the thriving plant life that breaks its way through the rocky and often arid ground.

The foreground is the more level and open, but still rough, defunct quarry. There John played hide-and-seek and a variety of imaginative games with his schoolmates. On the right, in the old abandoned rock quarry, sits a little bird near a crystal-clear pool. In the center rising to the top of the ikon is a bare rocky hilltop with a small hut for pilgrims

close to the summit. On the left is the top of a tree covered knoll. Rising into the early morning light are a number of rugged olive trees. They were initially sketched during a visit John made to California. In ancient biblical tradition, the olive tree was believed the tree of life in the Garden of Eden.

In his depiction of what first appears to be a purely natural setting, John is drawing upon ancient traditions expressed in the Bible and by spiritual writers in 7th Century Byzantium (when Christian iconography began to flourish). These spiritual writers firmly believed that the natural world has an inner spiritual dimension revealing the presence of God. Both in the Psalms and other biblical books, we often find a description of all of creation giving voice to the praise and glory of God. Some spiritual writers of that period insisted that a more complete understanding of the mysterious nature of God's presence in the universe requires us to recognize and revere both the natural world and sacred scripture as co-equal sources of divine revelation. (*Exegesis and Spiritual Pedagogy in Maximus the Confessor, pp. 100-108*)

To reveal the supernatural presence of God at work in the universe, the ikon's focus shifts from the natural world to the manifestation of God's presence in the uncreated Fire of the Holy Spirit, represented in the Fire on the mountain top descending from above. Nature itself, even with all its grandeur and awesome power, cannot free itself from bondage to the forces of death and destruction. Descending first upon the Apostles in Jerusalem, and then ultimately extending to all of creation, the Fire of the Holy Spirit marks the beginning of a new creation of Heaven and Earth, when all shall be reconciled, and death and sorrow are no more.

Above and surrounding the rocky hilltop, John crafts a mysterious fire with a remarkable diversity of colors. For several years, John struggled to represent the Fire of the Holy Spirit as emerging from the wood on the ground. Then in a work by John's Holy Cross friend and fellow artist, Br. Jeremiah, entitled "Fire in the Sky," John realized that the Fire of the Holy Spirit had to come from above, not as emerging from sticks on the ground. The colors of the fire are an exact reproduction of Br. Jeremiah's depiction of this Fire in the sky. We see this mysterious uncreated Fire of the Holy Spirit descending from the left onto and surrounding the rocky hilltop, in unusual shapes and blends of colors—red, gold, white, and blue.

In the foreground to the left, we see a little girl in a red dress with her left arm raised up to heaven. In her right hand she holds a broken piece of a colorful Easter piñata over the small stack of firewood at her feet. She is preparing to ignite the wood at her feet using a piece of the Easter piñata to bring the fire down from heaven onto the wood. *She is reaching up to heaven to call down the heavenly Fire of the Holy Spirit to achieve a transformation in the things of this world that nature itself cannot accomplish.*

She appears tiny in the large expanse of the natural landscape of the ikon. That she is physically small, a child, and female, all are central to the ikon's symbolism. She represents the still, small voice within, that is ultimately of vastly greater power and importance than the wild wind or raging fire or earthquake. *(Cf. I Kings 19:11-12)* By her gentleness she is destined to shake the world.

The Baptism of the Fire of the Holy Spirit offers a universal apostolic mission to all, a mission in no way limited or hindered by gender or littleness. The opposite is true. True greatness in the Gospels is something utterly different than this-worldly conceptions, with all their distortions of what is truly important in our world.

The little girl is a reminder that each of us has an apostolic calling as a child of God. We are called not only to experience the fire of God's love and mercy at work in us, but also to a firm personal resolve to share with others that redemptive force at work in our daily lives.

As Mary, the Blessed Mother of the Lord of all Creation, proclaims in her Magnificat (*Luke 1:46-55*)

> *My soul proclaims the greatness of the Lord...*
>
> *He has shown the strength of his arm,*
> *He has scattered the proud in their conceit.*
>
> *He has cast down the mighty from their thrones,*
> *And has lifted up the lowly.*
>
> *He has filled the hungry with good things,*
> *And the rich he has sent empty away.*

Directly behind the little girl, we see a simple gate made of wooden sticks. It opens a path for the religious pilgrim who has seen and now must act. The path guides the pilgrim up the mountain, winding past a grotto with a marble crucifix to the simple hut near the top of the mountain.

For John, the calling of fire down from heaven also recalls the fiery descent of the Holy Spirit upon the Disciples at Pentecost, enabling them to share the Gospel in all the languages of the earth. It also calls to my mind the vivid transition from darkness to the light of Christ's resurrection, symbolized by the lighting of the Easter Candle during the Easter Vigil Liturgy. I see that little girl, with her arm reaching up for the Fire in heaven, as waiting, like an Easter candle, for the Fire of God's love to come down and gently fill her heart, that she also may become *a light to the world*.

O Lord, we all experience the tangled growth of the true
and the false, of the good and the evil in our hearts.
Grant us true repentance.
Send the Fire of the Holy Spirit,
light our paths that daily we may turn from evil and
be grounded ever more deeply in all that is eternally
True, Beautiful, and Good.
Through Christ our Lord.

John Cobb's

CHAPEL IKONS

Group II

Biblical Figures and Themes

MARY AS A LITTLE GIRL

36" x 36"

1984

4

THE SPIRITUAL PREPARATION OF MARY AS A CHILD

The little girl on the pony, wearing blue jeans, a pink checkered shirt, and cowboy boots, is Marissa, a Hispanic girl from East Austin. Her blue robe designates her as representing Mary, the chosen one, who was to become the Mother of God. The man standing at the pony's head is José Mendiola, a man from Durango, Mexico. He is representing Joachim, Mary's father.

José and John worked side by side digging the thorn-laden mesquite from farmers' fields near the Colorado River east of Austin. Frosty, the white pony, was borrowed from John's neighbor.

A principal goal of John's ikons is to represent common human experiences shared by the key figures in salvation history, such as Mary,

Jesus' mother, and all other human beings across the ages, including our contemporaries.

As Mary was intimately to know human griefs and sorrows, so was little Marissa. Her parents had just gone through a divorce and one can see the grief in her eyes. Both little Marissa and little Mary also received tender care from those who loved them, and had enjoyable experiences such as sitting on a pony, or in Mary's case as a young girl, more likely a donkey.

A broader theme is on how God may be equipping each of us, often in tender and gentle ways, to deal with the demanding, thorn-laden tasks that we will face in the often tearful journeys of this life.

The hardest human work is more often interior than exterior. It requires a compassion, love and faithfulness stronger than death.

For this Mary is our model, excelling all others.

Even when the unimaginable happens to her, even when a sword pierces her own heart, the Blessed Mother remains constant in faith, hope, and love. Even as Jesus' male disciples were fleeing in terror when he was mocked, scourged and crucified, it was Mary and the other women who remained steadfastly by him.

She was there as he made his anguished journey through the streets of Jerusalem to Golgotha. She was there at the foot of his cross as he breathed his last.

How can one enter into Mary's world as Jesus' mom, to grasp, to understand something of what she humanly experienced and suffered? Is Mary simply thrown with no preparation into the inconceivable events of the Annunciation, in Bethlehem with no place to give birth except in a stable, the journey into Egypt fleeing those who sought the death of her child, the loss of Jesus as a young boy in the crowded, tumultuous and violent city of Jerusalem, her experience during Jesus' public ministry of teaching and healing in Galilee, his crucifixion and resurrection?

How does God help to prepare her for all the joyful, sorrowful, glorious and luminous mysteries she is to experience? How is God preparing each of us?

As it begins with Mary, it will also begin with us. It is the greatest of blessings to encounter, to be open to and nourished by God's grace in our lives. God initially prepares and strengthens Mary uniquely through her Immaculate Conception. But it doesn't stop there.

We are seldom thrown into situations of great importance without some forewarning. It is a gracious act of God to give his servants some premonition. The little girl Marissa riding the pony is a symbol of the far more desperate journey Mary shall make with the newborn Jesus on her flight to Egypt, with Joseph by her side.

This ikon is an imaginative presentation of God preparing Mary even as a little girl, when she is most secure, delightfully and fully in life, cared for by others' tenderness and love. Little Marissa now becomes little Mary, sitting on a gentle old pony, with her father Joachim by its head, and her little dog sitting at the pony's feet, devotedly looking up at her little mistress.

Prominent in the upper right corner, jutting out towards the back of Mary's head, is a cut thorn-laden mesquite branch. Her father Joachim cut it to provide his beloved daughter safe passage through the thorns.

Even within this tranquil domestic scene, the anxiety reflected in little Marissa's eyes are understood by John as representing the anxieties in little Mary's eyes, when God may have been preparing her,

granting her a premonition, even as a child, of the suffering that is to come— the fearful flight into Egypt, mounted on a donkey, with the newborn Jesus in her arms and Joseph leading the way, fleeing from Herod's servants who are seeking to find and kill her newborn child. (*Matthew 2:13-18*)

But we also see in her face and eyes a determination, a full resolve, by God's grace, to deal with whatever comes. She's ready for this journey.

MS. ROSE:

An Ikon of Christ

36" x 36"

1984

5

MS. ROSE:

AN IKON OF CHRIST

She worked as a janitor at the Department of Public Safety office on North Lamar in Austin, Texas, for nearly twenty years. For five years, John worked as a fellow janitor by her side. She cleaned the bathrooms; he did the floors.

The function of the ikon is to make visible the words of the Lord through images.

This particular ikon is making visible the role of the Christian saint as the role of servanthood, the most Christ-like image in the one most willing to stoop down and wash feet. (*John 13:1-17*) Ms. Rose washed public bathrooms daily for nearly twenty years—a very close fit.

The ikon of Ms. Rose moves beyond a simple verbal expression of piety—"Yes, she is serving the Lord." It moves us into a virtual direct physical encounter with this strong woman of great dignity who suffered much and spent the daily hours of her working life year after year in humble service of others' most basic needs. She was physically serving not merely the Department of Public Safety but also the people of Texas, whom the members of the Department also served.

Her image is an ikon, a sacred image of Christ, the Godhead still physically in our midst, who comes, not to be served, but to serve.

MANGER & SACRIFICE:
Room Between Heaven & Earth
36" x 36"
1989

6

Manger Scene & the Meaning of Sacrifice:
Room Between Heaven & Earth

Sometimes what we think we see and what is really going on are painfully disparate.

This ikon lays out before us what seems a tranquil agrarian scene. We see an elderly man bent over, wearing glasses, his left hand resting on the head of a black calf, a pipe in his right hand. In the background, the small figure of an elderly woman opens the door to the cattle shed.

The black mother cow on the right dominates the foreground. The shine in the cow's eyes, the sheen of her exquisitely detailed black face, neck and shoulder are stunning.

Anyone who knows the usual look of black egg tempera should be stunned. Black tempera is very flat, no sheen at all. John achieved the desired effect with patient and time-consuming multiple applications of the tempera with a knife and hours of hand polishing with soft cheese cloth.

Everything, including the rusty coil of baling wire on a fence post in the foreground, the weeds, a fence rail, the ground, the light and shadows on the metal roofed shed, all are crafted with luminous three-dimensional realism.

The couple were John's elderly neighbors. The husband ran a small cow/calf operation with around twenty-five head. John knew them well over many years and helped them in a variety of ways, including feeding the cows.

When John began his art studies at St. Edward's University, the couple provided him a free place to live in a shed on their farm in exchange for his labor. The woman is crippled. After her husband's death John became one of her principal care givers.

The calf has been selected to go to auction. The cow has been bred and a new calf has begun its life within her. They need room for the new calf and cash to supplement their meager income. John will load such calves into the trailer and take them to the sale barn.

Years ago, when I first saw this ikon in John's and Tina's home, I couldn't take my eyes off it. I've also worked in Ag and with lots of cows. I was captivated. But when John began explaining the spiritual importance of this ikon for him, everything I had been seeing and thinking in my reading of it was turned upside down.

What fundamentally changed everything were John's simple words that *this work had spiritually opened the door for him to the primitive meaning of sacrifice.*

This meaning is vividly present in every Ag operation and in the natural world, if we can open our eyes to it. Sacrifice is everywhere in our world, and often bloody. Most of what is produced in agricultural operations must be cut down, uprooted, or killed to release its blessings.

This is a corollary of a basic truth in nature that every living thing must eat to live and every living thing will be eaten. Every physical aspect of us eventually will be stripped away and merged with something else. Our skin will be stripped from our flesh, our flesh from our bones, and our bones themselves will disintegrate into dust. The naïve and neophytes to the Ag business seldom if ever reflect seriously on such things.

When the natural instinctual awareness of what is really going on is wakened, it can be a shock. Some eventually are able to see, understand, and even affirm their own necessary participation in these sacrifices.

Christians believe even the Creator of all things has chosen to be sacrificed in human form as the highest and most appropriate expression of *God's redeeming love for all of creation*. Others are horrified, unable to move beyond their biologically instinctual fear and revulsion.

Ann Voskamp, *New York Times* best-selling author and farmer's wife, graphically expresses this ancient and fundamental truth about sacrifice in her work: *The Broken Way: A Daring Path Into The Abundant Life*.

John skillfully uses egg tempera and gold leaf to flesh out the concrete details that embody the universal theme of sacrifice in nature and human life. Through the skillful use of words, Ann crafts concrete physical details embodying the same universal truth.

> "The farmer comes in from the barn, leaves a bucket from the henhouse at the back door with his boots. I can hear him washing up at the mudroom's porcelain sink. He steps into the kitchen. I look up from the dishes. He's seen it already. The man can read my eyes better than he reads the skies. Sometimes all our unspoken broken speaks louder than anything we could ever say. He reads my slow breaking over the kids lightning bolt news and all my not-enoughness that I can't even grope through the pain to find words for.
>
> He pulls me into himself, enfolds me. And then into the quiet he says it so soft I almost miss it, what I have held on to more than a thousand times since.

'You know—everything all across this farm says the same thing, you know that, right?' He waits till I let him look me in the eye, let him look into me and all this fracturing. 'The seed breaks to give us the wheat. The soil breaks to give us the crop, the sky breaks to give us the rain, the wheat breaks to give us the feast. There was once even an alabaster jar that broke to give him all the glory.' He looks right through the cracks of me. He smells of the barn and the dirt and the sky... He says it slowly like he means it: 'Never be afraid of being a broken thing.'"
(as cited in *Magnificat*, Aug 2018, Vol 20, No 6, pp. 136-137)

So it is, that the Christ, the Messiah who is Redeemer of All, had as his crib a manger used for feeding animals. And on the night he was betrayed, he took bread, *gave thanks*, broke it, and gave it to his disciples, saying, "Take and eat, this is my body, this is my blood."

Then out he went into the night, and once for all, conquering death for all, freely offered up his eternally efficacious, cruel and bloody, and life-giving sacrifice on the cross.

HOLY FAMILY BENEATH A TENT

34" x 34"

2016

HOLY FAMILY BENEATH A TENT

As I was "writing" this ikon, the idea of expressing pure family dedication mainly drew from the roots of an immense distress—divorce, infidelity, the life-long bitter breakup of my parents before me. These things seemed to go beyond mere impediment to widespread curse.

These clues to me were set in firm but terrible reality: the adultery and concupiscence of people reflected in the Old Testament book of Hosea. Hosea's call to maintain his fidelity to his unfaithful wife mirrored the merciful relation of a loving God to a faithless people.

My turmoil at dealing with wanton people inclined to death, my own inclination to blame and lapse into self-righteousness were pitiable conditions. I came to know how God was calling me beyond this in a very first-hand way.

In my distress I came to form an ideal. Family life is exceedingly complex, sometimes easily destroyed, often amazingly resilient. To me though, it would have to be a relationship dependent on grace. Joseph made that step and was directed through all the turns of his and Mary's life to a fabulously great end. St. Joseph is portrayed in the ikon as the provider. He is in the background, fishing.

What I wanted to start with was the idea that the picture would be an imaginary reflection of their being on vacation. That is how it began, that they might somehow be exonerated from these things. The reality is quite different, of course. They encountered tragedy, desperation, social pressures, threats on the child, and finally his suffering and death.

Jesus sits on Mary's lap. His cousin, John the Baptist, is the infant on her right with his right hand on her lap. He is wearing water shoes and perched on a crab float. Tina, my wife, is on the left in an expression of grief.

Her dad recently died, on Good Friday, actually. Her sadness, the pole that abruptly juts toward her head, is all meant to signify our distress and our hope to accept it. On the upper left, just under the blue tent, hanging from the cross-railing and post, is a much used and repaired family radio, held together with duct tape.

Even though this is a vacation and joyful, still there is a premonition of death. This will strike Mary, too, with the death of her son. On the right is a homeless man, John, who desperately wanted to be portrayed in something good. He hangs in repentance beneath the guillotine of becoming only a number (a broken intra-costal marker). An angel places a hand upon his shoulder; a modern radio plays their music.

Though perhaps not initially evident to the viewer, this ikon presents us with the central paradox of the Christian faith.

The eternal, omnipotent creator of all things has chosen to lay aside his almightiness and to become *Immanuel*, God with us, in the flesh of a tender, helpless, and utterly dependent infant. In Jesus' adult life God reduces himself to the role of a servant, even stooping down to wash his disciples' feet. *(John 13:1-17)* His earthly ministry ends culminating with rejection by those he came to serve and with his brutal death upon the cross.

Jesus the Messiah, God's chosen one, came among us not as a deliverer wielding the power of the sword. He comes humbly, reduced to servitude, and subject like us to the powers of time and death. *(Philippians 2:5-9)* He comes as God with us, not to coerce submission but to break upon our hearts and minds with the light of God's tender mercies. In this God humbly manifests the mystery of his unquenchable thirst for our love for him, and also for us to share this same love with one another, especially the most vulnerable among us.

Saint Teresa of Calcutta powerfully expresses this humble, incomprehensible mystery of the eternal and omnipotent God's love for each of us illumined in in the light of the Christ's crying out in thirst from the cross:

> "I thirst," Jesus said on the cross when he was deprived of every consolation, dying in absolute Poverty, left alone, despised and broken in body and soul. He spoke of His thirst—not for water—but for love and sacrifice. *(Mother Teresa, p 41)*

> His ways are so beautiful—to feel that we have God almighty to stoop so low as to love you and me and to make use of us—and make us feel that he really needs us. As I grow older my wonder at His humility grows not for what He gives but for what He is— the Bread of Life—*The Hungry one. (Mother Teresa, p. 273)*

In John's ikon of the Holy Family, an ordinary human family is camped under a tent on the beach. It was within a family just such as this, 2,000 years ago, that the eternal, omnipotent God chose to dwell, in the flesh of a human baby utterly dependent upon its mother's care. Though invisible in his own divine and eternal nature, God chose in his tender mercies to become visible to us in time, fully present and incarnate in the human flesh of Jesus the Christ, the eternal Father's only begotten son, for the salvation of all.

The ikon is a reflection on the tragedy, desperation, social pressures, threats on the child, and finally his suffering and death; it is also a reflection on how the outreach of God's compassion and mercy can also be experienced within ordinary family life. God's mercy is concretely represented by the tent covering the Holy Family. This is a biblical symbol, frequently used in the Old Testament, of the covering and protection provided by God's mercy and love. The outreach of the angel, tenderly placing her hand on the shoulder of the homeless man, also is a manifestation of the tender mercies of God.

There is unspeakable cruelty and suffering in our world, but also hundreds of millions of human beings are God's angels of mercy across the globe, actively reaching out selflessly and in sacrificial ways to those in need. We are free to choose which focus we allow to guide our own energies and lives.

The life of the Holy Family, properly seen and understood, gives courage, hope, and strength to all those committed to the spiritual journey of life, even in the midst of suffering, to an ever greater, more tender and all including good.

On the cross, Jesus lifts up and takes into himself all the human suffering poured out across the ages; in his resurrection all with even the slightest inclination towards what is truly good, will experience transformation through his almighty power into a fullness of joy that shall never pass. This is a joy we can also directly experience in faith even now in all the limitations of this life.

Lord Jesus, may your love unite
Us all in bonds of endless light, bringing
Household peace, may you overcome
Life's woes in every earthly home.

JESUS FALLS THE 3RD TIME:

9th Station of the Cross

17" x 36"

2005

8

JESUS FALLS THE 3RD TIME:

9TH STATION OF THE CROSS

This ikon is chock full of the interior and exterior barriers confronting all Christians even as they are actively seeking to respond to the challenge of Christ: *Pick up your cross and follow me.*

The religious brother in the foreground is standing alongside the cross, as Christ falls for the third time. He has not fled the scene as the disciples did, but his anguish at the sight of the fallen Jesus under the weight of his cross is emotionally too much for him. In the horror of this moment even the good man looks away.

In his refusal to flee the scene he is present with Christ on the way of the cross. He is also sharing Christ's experience in the Garden of Gethsemane before his arrest and condemnation to death on the cross. There, greatly distressed and troubled, Christ falls to the ground weeping and praying that if it were possible this hour might pass from him. "Yet not what I will but what you will." (*Mark 14:32-36*)

In the ikon of Jesus being taken down from the cross, we see the left hand and wrist of this same religious brother reaching up to help take Jesus down.

Look carefully at the eyes of the strong burly man reaching toward the cross. He wants to pick it up and looks intently, beseechingly at the religious brother. He needs some authoritative sign that he should in fact pick up the cross. But it is hard for him to do this on his own. He

is looking for an authority figure to tell him what to do. But the authority figure of the religious brother is looking away. The strong man is looking directly at him seeking affirmation that he should step forward and help Jesus carry his cross.

Instead, the religious brother shields his eyes to avoid looking directly into his eyes. Directly behind the Brother (in line with the tree) is a man wearing a red scarf, looking on in a rather circumspect way. He is puzzled by the terrible price Jesus was willing to pay challenging the established religious authority of the Pharisees and Sadducees.

You might notice the two men further in the rear with their backs towards us. Both men wear uniforms, the less obvious one somewhat clandestine—and perhaps a bit undercover. They are exterior barriers present to keep Mary and the other faithful women from getting too close to Jesus. The repulsed followers are not just women but Black women, and the guards are Mississippi ferry guards. St. John is there with Mary and the other women, barely visible, farthest back on the right, observant, praying, witnessing everyone's reactions.

Jesus, fallen under the weight of his cross, looks only at the earth. His hands and knees on the ground, he is entirely focused on completing the sacrifice that conquers death. He is ready for death and burial, melting into the ground. The blood from his wounds seeps into the earth.

Jesus is the powerful cosmic seed that dying and falling into the earth, will rise again and raise all creation with him.

THE LIFTING UP UPON THE CROSS

17" x 36"

2004

9

JESUS LIFTED UP
ON THE CROSS

Ikons 9 and 10 are a good illustration of how John's work progresses and develops reflectively even as he is working on it. Initially he thought of the two ikons as depictions of the same scene, of Christ being taken down from the cross. Ikon 9 depicted the darkness in the scene and ikon 10 the light. But as he continued to work and meditate on the two ikons, it gradually became clear to him that they are best viewed as a paired dynamic sequence. The lifting up on the cross is a scene of darkness and chaos. The theme of taking down from the cross is touched with the beginnings of a hope-filled dawn. Each stands in an intimate and necessary relation to the other.

Lifting up on the cross is dominated by the darkened sky in the background. We see Jesus crucified with two criminals. The cross on the right is already raised, the criminal's face and outstretched arms in darkness. The other criminal crashes to the ground under the weight of his cross, directly beneath Jesus. In the left foreground Jesus is lifted up on his cross. We are able to see only part of his face and chest, left shoulder and arm still in the light.

The black person with the white head cloth represents Simon of Cyrene, compelled by the Romans to carry Jesus' cross. (*Matthew 27:32*) It is believed Simon was a dark-skinned African man because the city of Cyrene was located in present day Libya. It is presumed he traveled to Jerusalem to celebrate the Passover. With one hand firmly on top of the cross and the other underneath, he controls its weight and lifts it. His eyes shut, his face downcast, disconsolate.

He is compelled against his will by those with the power of the sword to be their instrument in Jesus' crucifixion. The jagged broken end of the cross bar ascending over his head symbolizes oppression. A lighter-skinned man with glasses, whose face we barely see, raises his arms and hands from behind and over Simon, straining to push the cross upward.

The scene is a jumble of darkness, desolation, and death.

THE TAKING DOWN FROM THE CROSS:
13th Station of the Cross
17" x 36"
2003

10

Jesus Taken Down from the Cross:

13th Station of the Cross

The dark clouds are scattering and faint traces of blue sky beginning to emerge, all intimations of the resurrection. The man on the left beholds his crucified Lord with unutterable grief. Yet Jesus' body is bathed in light, his passion complete, his suffering done.

His brokenness is lifted up by tendrils reaching down from heaven above, his body taken down by caring, loving hands and hearts below.

THE SEEN AND THE UNSEEN
47" x 36"

2014

11

THE SEEN AND THE UNSEEN

This is a symbolically intricate, dynamic, and complex ikon. Possessing great psychological depth, it is alive with conflicting, battling, yet interdependent forces, with the wreckage strewn everywhere across the floor.

Divided into four quadrants, two on the vertical plane and two on the horizontal, the top represents heaven, the eternal and the unseen. The lower half symbolizes the visible chaos of this world where things are incessantly coming into being and perishing.

The bottom left and right quadrants depict two archetypically different ways human beings approach life. On the left are romantics who explore life chiefly through passion, direct experience, and feelings. On the right are the intellectuals, scholarly types, exploring through reason, logic, and books. The first are frequently associated with southern regions and the romance languages; the second with the peoples and languages of northern Europe.

On both sides of the center horizontal line of the ikon we see two men being crucified. Jesus the Redeemer is on the right. On the left is the repentant thief whom Jesus has assured will be in paradise that very day. The two figures represent the point of transition from the chaos, disorder, suffering and death of the visible world to the unseen deathless harmony and joy of heaven.

The visible disorder of this world is depicted by the profusion of scattered clutter littering the bottom half of the ikon. The world is a workshop filled with the scattered detritus of our labors. The ikon also depicts the clutter and disorder in John's studio where most of these luminous works came to life, including this one.

The organizing theme as a whole is that the unseen, eternally loving and merciful Creator never abandons his visible creation. Multiple symbols represent the continuous, never ceasing, divine outreach.

Top center is a red, blue, and black circle, supported by a winged angel on the bottom left. Inside the circle is a woman. She is crouched inside the ring, feet firmly planted on both sides, and reaches out to Jesus on his cross.

The circle itself is a traditional symbol of the infinite which cannot be seen. John sees the woman in the circle as representing "the Spiritual Mother," applying first to the biblical Sarai, Abraham's wife, whose name God changed to Sarah.

Later in the New Testament this comes to be more concretely Mary, the mother of Jesus. She is surrounded by the Jewish symbolic chain of ancestry and is reaching down to claim the Son. Her dark mantle is being torn from her to reveal the gown of spring and the intimation of resurrection.

Beneath the circle is a large golden square made up of intersecting horizontal and vertical lines. It is a Russian ikon carved in gold, symbolically representing the invisible heavenly temple descending to earth.

A square picture of beautiful yet still unredeemed nature seems almost to float with no visible support squarely in the center of the golden ikon of the temple. The small white figure in the center is the Lamb of God who takes away the sin of the world.

Everything is in process, not yet completed. It is as though the unseen is patiently waiting to enfold and transform a beautiful and fully redeemed nature. This is the biblical promise of the creation of a new heaven and a new earth.

There the powers of death and sorrow are no more, and everything, absolutely everything in heaven and on earth is reconciled. (*Ephesians 1: 9-10; Colossians 1: 19-20*)

In the left lower quadrant we see the romantic with feet wide apart standing energetically before us. His hands are outstretched in adoration, eyes intently focused on the Blessed Mother in the heavenly Circle above reaching out to her beloved son. The individual in this scene is Richard, who lives with John and his wife Tina. He's a principal caretaker of Jesse, John's beloved, handicapped brother-in-law. His eyes and heart and body are reaching out to the Blessed Mother in the circle above. Richard lost his own mother when he was only six years old.

In the right lower quadrant, in vivid contrast to the romantic, is the scholar and deep thinker. He is sitting comfortably in a chair at the very foot of the cross. His left hand relaxed on his left knee, his face indifferently turned away from the crucified Lord directly before him.

All his attention is turned to a book resting on a dolly on the floor to his right. His right hand reaches down to crack it open. The dolly represents the enormous volume and weight of all the books that have captured most of his attention throughout his life.

In the lower right hand corner we see a bit of an orange ladder. It represents the futile human attempt to climb up to heaven without God's grace.

The archetypes of two distinct ways of seeking truth are not to be interpreted simplistically. A balanced person needs both. Both are present in romance languages and northern European cultures. But one archetype can dominate a particular person. Who has not heard book learning demeaned in contrast to the real world of direct experience. This also works the other way round. We all know individuals scornful and dismissive of those with little formal education.

We encounter both extremes in our daily lives. Yet both romantic and more analytical approaches have important roles to play in a fruitful spiritual journey. Abundant practical experience, powerful feelings and our unexamined preconceptions can blind us to deeper truths that only careful thinking, study and reflection reveal. And book learning not complemented by direct, hands on experience is often shallow and superficial.

The ikon is suggesting a more balanced spiritual path amidst the chaos of this world.

Heaven and earth are depicted as essentially interconnected because from the very beginning the first is the divinely intended destiny of the second. What we learn on our earthly pilgrimage is necessary to prepare us for heaven.

Throughout this journey there will be heavenly influences seeking to guide our spiritual path. As Shakespeare reminds us, "There is a divinity that shapes our ends rough hew them how he may." The reverse is also true that rough hew our ends how we may, still God shapes them to fulfill his purposes. For it is God's desire "that all be saved and come to knowledge of the truth." (*I Timothy 2:4*)

Reason, thought, study, and reflection pursued in the right way can enrich rather than diminish passion, feeling, and direct experience. Each can provide correction and guidance to the other. Working together, intellectual wisdom and passion provide guided strength and needed correction to each other. It requires a sustained commitment to work hard at developing ears truly able to hear, eyes truly able to see and a heart truly able to understand.

Our pilgrimage in life from the seen to the unseen always has its beginning in the free gift of divine grace. But our life cannot grow in fruitfulness apart from individually chosen spiritual discipline and work. We need actively to seek out rich and nourishing food both for mind and heart on our arduous journeys through the often dark, tearful valleys of this world.

ST. PETER'S PRAYER OF REPENTANCE

17" x 36"

1985

St. Peter's Prayer of Repentance

St. Peter is Mr. Brown, a water well driller and plumber from New Mexico.

The ikon depicts a balding grey-bearded workman with glasses as St. Peter, driven to his knees in a bed of flowering thistles. A rock by his side signifies his name, and a halo floats over him. Two streaks of blood in the upper left recall Peter's martyrdom on an upside down cross.

When John asked Mr. Brown for permission to paint him as representing St. Peter, the man immediately, spontaneously, dropped to his knees in prayer.

The principal theme is Peter's repentance after betraying Jesus. This is easily said. What is far more challenging is to reach a deeper understanding of the freeing power of Peter's repentance.

The writing of ikons is how John works spiritually to reach this deeper wisdom. He also works with the hope that at least some of the fruits of this labor can be positively shared with others.

A critical moment in John's crafting of this ikon lay in his sudden recognition of a very different symbolism of the rock. It could also symbolize the rock that an angry Moses struck to provide water for an angry Israelite people dying of thirst in the desert.

John immediately grasped that the emotional and spiritual effects flowing from authentic repentance are dramatically different than those flowing from anger. The water from the rock in the desert struck in anger provided the people only what was required to survive physically.

Peter's prayer of repentance dealt with a spiritual reality of an entirely different order. His moral and spiritual shame stemmed from the fact that he had cowardly made the issue of his own physical survival more important than his fidelity to the person he loved more than any other.

In betraying Jesus, and the message and mission Jesus entrusted to him, he was betraying all that he knew truly to be good.

Authentic repentance always involves three things: heartfelt contrition, contempt for sin, and resolution to amend one's life. All of these we see in Peter and in the fact that subsequently he was steadfast and accepted even bloody martyrdom to remain faithful to his Lord.

We believe it was Peter's capacity still to focus on the goodness of Jesus' person and mission, rather than his own betrayal, that gave his prayer of repentance its great spiritual depth.

No doubt he initially felt immense anger towards himself. But somehow he was able to regain his spiritual bearings and focus yet again on the mission Jesus had entrusted to him. This is the mission of leadership in a religious community committed to sharing God's love and mercy for all.

It is a mission that could never be fulfilled through acts of anger.

This required him, no less in his relationship with himself than in his relationship with others, to move beyond anger and resentment to mercy and forgiveness.

Authentic religious repentance is quite different than what we usually see happening around and within us. It progressively frees us both from the inner destructive powers of anger and also from outer patterns of behavior destructive to self and others. This requires an honest confrontation with our sins, deep contrition, and a continuous commitment day by day to doing all that is required to amend our lives.

These freedoms are not possible apart from wisdom, understanding and the self-acceptance growing from the healing powers of genuine repentance. This is the path St. Peter has chosen when driven to his knees in those thistles. He is now able to accept the mercy and compassion of God as infinitely greater than even his sin of betrayal and to amend his life accordingly.

The New Testament tells us:

> "You have heard that it was said to the men of old, "You shall not kill; and whoever kills shall be liable to judgment." But I say to you that everyone who is angry with his brother shall be liable to judgment."
>
> *(Matthew 5:21-23a)*

> "Know this, my beloved brethren... the anger of man does not work the righteousness of God."
>
> *(James 1:19-20)*

Judas, after his betrayal of Jesus, refused to dig deeper to find the wellsprings of repentance and forgiveness in the infinite love and mercy of God. Instead, in reaction to his great sin, he acted lethally in anger and despair against his own life, even as he had acted in anger and despair against Jesus' life. His corrupted heart and imagination refused to accept the spiritual challenge of changing his life. His angry, constricted and narrow focus only on himself left him unable even to imagine the possibility of a God of infinite mercy.

Peter somehow went deeper. Though a simple and uneducated working man Peter honestly confronted his terrible sin of betraying the Lord. He did not give up without digging deeper, plumbing the depths and getting to the bottom of things. Driven to his knees, deeply repentant, and committed to changing his life, he reached the rock of faith and opened his heart and mind to the sweet and reconciling wellsprings of the inexhaustible mercy, forgiveness, and love of God.

Father in heaven, when your strength takes possession of us
we no longer say: *Why are you cast down, my soul?*
So now that the surging waves of our indignation have passed
over us, let us feel the healing calm of your forgiveness.
Inspire us to yearn for you always, like the deer for running
streams, until you satisfy every longing in heaven.

Psalm Prayer, Week II, Monday, Morning Prayer,
Christian Prayer, 794

NATHANAEL

17" x 34"

2004

NATHANAEL

ow it must be that Nathanael stuck strong with Jesus, and how, because he is amongst the company that goes fishing after the resurrection. He is in the boat as Jesus calls out, "Children, have you caught anything?" This is the second time we hear about him, the first was when he was seen beneath a fig tree and was called to believe.

We ourselves long to have been in His presence, with all our hearts, with knowledge in hindsight of the entire perspective of His works and all the pageantry of the old and new, and the Holy Spirit to guide and bless, still, we just wish we had been on that beach and had breakfast with Him. What a work of incredible proportions.

It is not easy to ask someone about being available if they are outside your faith community. With fortune in hand, my sweet friend Claudia Goldman, a Catholic, was married to a New York Jewish man, Gary Goldman. So I asked her if her husband would pose as Nathanael.

There was only a minor disagreement: shall he be in praise or in contemplation? We opted for a book, the instrument of the intellect, and he took out his carefully wrapped tallit (tzitzit) and scullcap, and chose his shirt, like a golden city seen from above. The Book cradled in his hands represents all those sacred texts for which the Jewish people, time and again in their long and troubled history, risked their lives and shed their blood to preserve.

We were ready!

John Cobb's

CHAPEL IKONS

Group III

Saints in the Church

ST. FRANCIS AND BR. LEO

36" x 36"

2002

ST FRANCIS & BR. LEO IN THEIR EARTHEN HOVEL

St. Francis of Assisi (1181-1226) is founder of the Franciscan religious order, a powerful reform movement within the church during the Middle Ages. Franciscans continue their important spiritual work around the world today. Br. Leo was one of his early disciples and an important source for the earliest documents on the historical beginnings of this spiritual movement.

Jesus' beatitudes in the Gospels are the heart of St. Francis' spirituality:

> "Blessed are the poor... Blessed are those who mourn... Blessed are the meek... the merciful... the peacemakers... the persecuted..."
>
> *(Matthew 5)*

The ikon is a remarkably concrete, precisely crafted, and detailed depiction of the kind of primitive huts in which the earliest Franciscans often chose to dwell. To make the representation as realistic as possible, John first handbuilt the hut out of sticks, branches, vines, and other natural materials abundantly available on his three-acre tract. For added effect he also threw in an old abandoned gate and shutter. Then he tied the whole thing together using old, rusty discarded chicken wire.

The insets providing close up views of the hut help one to see the details. In the electronic version of the book one can really examine the details, magnifying specific sections of the ikon on a quality computer screen. Looking at John's work in this way is almost like a biologist using a microscope to examine nature. The closer you look, the more extraordinary details you see.

Beginning at the top left of the ikon is a small green canopy of leaves growing from rough vines rising up from their roots in the earth. The upwardly growing vines form a key part of the outer shell of the hut. This structure is filled in with a collection of interwoven vertical and horizontal sticks.

At the bottom in the foreground is an old discarded shutter used to complete the lower part of a side wall. In the front on the left is an old abandoned gate used as the entrance. Discarded and bent chicken wire is used to help hold the structure together.

We catch just a glimpse of Br. Leo; his ashen face, a pale left hand against his check, appears on the far left, just above the top of the abandoned shutter, close to and facing outward toward the discarded gate. He is consumed by sorrow and could be described as singing the blues.

The reproduction of the ikon's full image at the beginning of this meditation is too small to see St. Francis clearly. He is to the right of Leo, hidden deep within the darkness of the same earthen hovel in which they both live, but Francis draws light and life from an utterly different spiritual place.

The challenge presented the reader of this ikon is to move from the dark and jumbled externals it graphically depicts to the interior spiritual dynamic going on within that hovel.

The central dynamic becomes visible only through a thoughtful examination of the contrasts between the face and posture of Leo and that of Francis. Though still challenging, these elements are perceptible when viewing the actual ikon, while the much smaller scale of the photographic image conceals them. The inset zooming in on the interior of the hut and St. Francis' face provides more detail.

As we move from the exterior to the interior, what had seemed dark and confusing becomes luminously simplified. Francis' face is rapt in contemplation of a small golden crucifix, suspended from the top right of the hut, the fingers of his right hand outstretched in spiritual ecstasy.

Symbolically, the hut is more than a hut. It represents not only our embodiment but also our entrapment in all the interwoven and entangled complexities of our paradoxical universe—spiritual, material, and biological.

Yet even in the midst of the entangling darkness and destructive powers of this world, Francis is able to see the light, the beauty, the healing goodness at work in all of God's creation.

Why can Francis see this beauty, goodness and healing power, and Leo cannot? Why is Francis rapt in joy and Leo deep in sorrow, his back turned both on Francis and the simplifying power of the cross that is the source of Francis' joy?

Francis, enabled by the gratuitous gift of divine grace, has penetrated more deeply than Br. Leo into the central mystery and joy of the Christian faith, the mystery of the freeing and redemptive power of the cross.

Apart from the freely chosen loving embrace of this paradoxical mystery, it is not possible either to understand or fully to live the truth of Christianity.

For Christians immersed in the eucharistic mystery and opening their hearts to the intensity visible in Francis' face and his outstretched hand, it is as though one hears Francis himself affirming through his life what is daily proclaimed by the faithful at celebrations of the Eucharist:

> *Save us, Savior of the world, for by your Cross and Resurrection you have set us free.*

Francis took literally Jesus' words, "pick up my cross and follow me." This was his mantra for his followers. He wanted them, as much as spiritually possible, to walk in the very foot prints of Jesus.

In 1926 when Pope Pius XI commemorated the seventh centenary of the death of St. Francis, he wrote,

> ... While it is presumptuous to make comparisons between the
> heroes of sanctity... still it would appear that in no one has
> the image of Christ our Lord, and the ideal of Gospel life, been
> more faithfully and strikingly expressed than in Francis. For this
> reason, while he called himself 'the Herald of the Great King,'
> he has been justly styled 'the second Christ,' because he appeared
> like Christ reborn to his contemporaries no less than in later
> ages, with the result that he lives today in the eyes of men and
> will live unto posterity.

Among all the saints of post-apostolic times, it is generally conceded, none seems to have exercised a more profound influence upon the Church and the world, not only in his own age, but also during the subsequent centuries down to our own day, than the Little Poor Man of Assisi. None had and still has so many devoted followers and ardent admirers within the fold of the Catholic Church as well as outside it. None has been the subject of so many biographies and other books, written and printed in every major language of the world. (*St Francis*, Foreword, p. v)

The heart of his religious rule of life was for the brothers "to follow the teachings and footsteps of Christ." (*St. Francis of Assisi*, pp. 7-8) A complete renunciation of self that led to a deep interior humility was the heart of their spiritual life.

> ... their following of Christ was not to be something purely external. It was to be an imitation of Christ that would lead to a total transformation interiorly, a complete submission of the spirit of the flesh to the spirit of Christ, a seraphic love of him who is *the way, and the truth, and the life. (John 14:6)*

Francis' father was a cloth merchant selling expensive goods to the wealthy of Assisi. He was training his son to take over this business after him. Francis' final break from the world was initiated early in 1206 in a radical confrontation with his earthly father.

> His ways just before this had greatly disturbed his father, Pietro Bernardone, particularly the fact that he had sold some bolts of cloth and had disposed of the money. In the hope of recovering the money and winning his son back from what he considered his errant ways, Francis' father cited him to appear before the civil authorities of Assisi. But Francis refused to appear there, on the plea that he had already entered the service of the Lord and was therefore no longer subject to civil officials. His father then cited him to appear before the bishop of Assisi instead. Francis respected this summons, and there, in the presence of his father and the bishop, he stripped off his garments and cast them at the feet of his father, saying, "From now on I can freely say Our Father who art in heaven, not father Peter Bernardone." (*St. Francis of Assisi*, p. 27)

In his 1221 Rule of Life the brothers were "to live in obedience, without property, and in chastity." (*St. Francis of Assisi,* pp. 31-42) They were forbidden to take money and commanded to care for the sick. Money could be accepted only for that purpose. They were to love one another and never malign or speak injuriously of one another. (*St. Francis of Assisi,* pp. 40-41) They were not to speak negatively about those who chose to live in affluence and material luxury. In their travels they are...

> ... to take nothing with them... neither staff, nor wallet, nor bread nor money (*Luke 9:3*) When they enter a house, they are to say first of all, Peace to this house (*Luke 10:5*). And they should remain in the same house, eating and drinking what they have (*Luke 10:7*).
>
> They should not offer resistance to injury; if a man should strike them on the right cheek, they should turn the other cheek also towards him (cf. *Matthew 5:39*) If a man would take away their cloak, they should not grudge him their coat along with it. They should give to every man who asks, and if a man takes what is theirs, they should not ask him to restore it (cf. *Luke 6:29-30*). (*St. Francis*, p. 42)

Francis' spiritual athleticism and capacity to endure pain joyfully, were beyond his followers' capabilities. Thus we see Leo singing the blues, with his face turned toward the exit and away from Francis and the liberating cross. This gap between lover and beloved is the well spring of the blues. Yet paradoxically, by singing the blues, Leo will also find the path that leads him out of them.

Although Leo has not yet achieved the level of spiritual insight and ecstasy of Francis, this does not mean that God has not also granted him an energy and spiritual wisdom and balance that Francis himself sometimes lacks. The irrepressible enthusiasms of zealously religious individuals can lead them to overstep the boundaries of what even God is asking of them. Then they need to be reined in.

Leo also experienced the blues dealing with this very different kind of challenge between himself and Francis. At times Leo believed Francis' extreme ways needed correction and more balance. His own spiritual integrity would not permit him to abandon these convictions. But apart from God's help it was not clear to him how he might help Francis to hear the truth of what he is seeking to share. This is disclosed in a wonderful story in the *Franciscan Omnibus of Sources* (*St. Francis of Assisi*, pp. 1320-1322):

How God Spoke to St. Francis Through Brother Leo

St. Francis tells Br. Leo:

> "Brother Leo... so as to spend the time praising God, I will say something and you must answer what I tell you, and be careful not to change my words. I will say this: 'Oh, Brother Francis, you have done so much evil and sin in the world that you deserve hell' – and you, Brother Leo, shall answer: 'It is true that you deserve the depth of hell.'"

Then the exchange begins with Francis time after time heaping abuse upon himself with the expectation that Leo would dutifully obey. "Yes brother, you are worthy of hell." But he doesn't. Instead Leo repeatedly responds as follows: "God will perform so much good through you that you will go to Paradise."

Francis protests insisting Leo must obey and repeat Francis' self-condemning words. Again and again Leo disobeys Francis' command; he responds with wonderfully positive words. Francis gets more and more exasperated. Finally, Br. Leo responds:

> "God... will exalt and glorify you for all eternity because 'whoever humbles himself shall be exalted' – 'and I cannot say anything else because God is speaking through my mouth...' And they stayed up until dawn in this humble contest, with many tears and great spiritual consolations."

IHS

Lord, make me an instrument of thy peace;
Where there is hatred
Let me sow love;
Where there is injury, pardon;
Where there is doubt, faith;
Where there is despair, hope;
Where there is darkness, light;
And where there is sadness, joy.

O DIVINE MASTER,
Grant that I many not so much seek
To be consoled as to console;
To be understood as to
Understand;
To be loved as to love;

For it is in giving that we receive;
It is in pardoning that we are pardoned
And it is in dying that we are born to eternal life.

This widely known prayer is often titled *The Prayer of St. Francis*, but it is a modern prayer that does not stem directly from his hand. It is a wonderful manifestation of how many important themes at the heart of St. Francis' spirituality still resonate in modern consciousness. The three letters in gold, *IHS*, above the prayer, are an ancient monogram of the name of Jesus. The first three letters in the original Greek of Jesus' name are the *iota, eta,* and *sigma,* represented in English as *ihs.*

OUR LADY OF GUADALUPE
17" x 34"
2011

15

OUR LADY OF GUADALUPE

Gabriela was administering the Eucharist at Our Lady of Guadalupe Church. She was a delicate girl with tiny hands, a slight speech impediment, a scar upon one cheek, she dreamed of being a dancer. Somehow she was viewed as insignificant, but public scrutiny was a passing phenomenon, it was those quiet courageous dark eyes so full of unrealized life and perhaps never quite fully seen by the hustling world that could not enter into that elemental meaning she offered. Someone said they had seen her serving hamburgers at Dan's.

It was in the quick glimpse of the eyes when she gave the host that one was able to recognize and apprehend this solemn moment—to see and be seen. The world may pass by and never know, but we who have received from this person shall humbly recognize its power, not to enslave, but to free. Long may she stand!

EL SANTO NIÑO:

The Holy Child

17" x 34"

2004

16

SANTO NIÑO DE ATOCHE

I had wanted to do something special for my wife's mom. She was a special devotee of the Santo Niño and she had an ancient print on very thin paper. It was near to tatters and with all the best intentions I sought to preserve the image. At the first hint of pva glue, it just disintegrated. What was I going to do now?

So I began the long process of reconstruction. I'll take the great grandson, I'll dress him in the outfit, I'll find a South American water gourd, the empty basket, of course (from having taken his mom's fresh bread to the poor in the morning). I'll find a great feather in the hat, and I'll throw in the dog (Chi-Chee-Loco) for good measure. Maybe she will be pleased. She had a special tiny dog named "Rocket," so there you go!

What I didn't like, though, about his normal presentation as a blue-eyed, blonde Spaniard, was the fact that he did not look at all like the people in whom he found such fervor of faith. Why would they revere so benevolently someone who really did not look like them at all? Can't we see ourselves in the faces of those we esteem? Perhaps we could identify more with the Saint if we made even a paltry attempt at recognizing our own genuine efforts to live out at least some of the goodness we admire in them.

These were the things I wanted to add to the already engaging story of the Christ-child, and as well, to include the possibility that they too could become Saints.

Tina's mom is Hispanic and I was taking liberties with what she desired in the image, desires that run very, very deep. She could only vaguely assent to a non-traditional image of the *Santo Niño* that depicted him looking like most Hispanic children.

John Cobb's

CHAPEL IKONS

Group IV

The Human Journey Into Goodness

MINISTRY TO THE WIDOW AND ORPHAN
17" x 36"
1987

MINISTRY TO THE WIDOW AND ORPHAN

The function of this ikon is to represent the verbal message of the New Testament letter of James about what it actually means to be religious.

"Religion that is pure and undefiled before God and the Father is this: to visit orphans and widows in their affliction, and to keep oneself unstained from the world."

James 1:27

It is not about establishing power over others, not subjecting oneself in sacrifice, not worship destined to lead to other worlds, but simply care and respect for powerless people.

MACHISMO AND FILIAL PIETY
17" x 36"
2006

18

MACHISMO AND FILIAL PIETY

The machismo of harsh and dominating male patriarchy flowing from the primitive craving for power and ego-gratification, brings alienation and deep trouble to men as well as to women and children. This holds true east, west, north or south, whether Anglo or Hispanic, religious or secular.

In this ikon we see the deep trouble depicted in the relation between a Hispanic grandfather and his granddaughter. It looks like the big and dominating patriarchal figure has all the power. The granddaughter is sitting submissively at his feet, below the patriarchal throne, in her candy striper hospital service uniform.

Neither looks the other in the face. They are sitting physically very close, yet so far apart.

As is usually the case with John's ikons, reading them involves a more penetrating spiritual reflection on what is happening than initially meets the eye.

In truth the granddaughter is the strong one and she will prevail. Her being and perspective are grounded in what is most important in life and will overcome. Her left hand is dropped down on a model of the church.

And the church, the bride of Christ, is feminine. This is distorted by an all-male, often machismo, hierarchy.

The granddaughter, who may seem passive and submissive, is in fact reaching down and drawing strength from the feminine heart of the church. From this she draws her spiritual oxygen and strength. Her candy striper hospital uniform speaks of her commitment to the loving care of others.

It is the spiritual strength of committed loving service and compassion that will prevail. This is the ultimate source of all forgiveness, healing and peace. At the end everything else will pass away. All of us will experience this at the end of our lives, when much we thought most important proves illusory and is stripped and taken away.

JOY: MY BROTHER-IN-LAW, JESSE SERANO

17" x 37"

2000

19

JOY:

MY BROTHER-IN-LAW, JESSE SERANO

Jesse was born on Christopher Columbus Day in 1966. He has an externally limited world caused by spinal meningitis when he was six months old. He cannot speak, walk, clean, or feed himself. The doctors were willing to let him die. His mother would not allow it and fought for him.

Tina still vividly remembers her mom's statement in the hospital. "I came here to give life, not to take it away." Jesse is now fifty-three years old.

Tina and John care for him in their home. Richard, a close Hispanic friend who lives with them, assists them. They find Jesse, as the day of his birth indicates, an explorer of his world. He is not passive. He actively investigates the things and people around him with an intense stare. For people not familiar with him, this can be disturbing. Jesse wants to figure out who this person is.

He has remarkable abilities to penetrate emotional dishonesty in how people sometimes attempt to relate to him. He also has a discerning ear for Tejano music. When it's authentic, he manifests his pleasure, when not, his strong disapproval. When given a picture of himself or his parents, he brings it up to his face and kisses it.

When visiting John and Tina, I often see Jesse outside in a wheel chair simply enjoying the sunshine and natural world of their little three acre farm. Sometimes they put out balloons or other colorful objects near him that dance in the wind, capturing his joyful attention.

Jesse's joy in life is not limited and it is something he shares. Even today, after his mother's passing, he contributes to the joy of the Cobb household. His physical form sitting cross-legged recalls the squatted form of the Buddha.

Tina, Jesse's sister, made the design and it was super-inscribed onto the painting.

The devoted, nurturing and loving care of Jesse by the Serrano and Cobb families is a herculean work of love. This kind of nurturing, faithful love, over fifty-three years, and the arduous labor it daily demands, is not humanly possible except as a work of divine grace.

It is the greatest of all possible miracles, greater even than the raising of the dead.

Only the divinely given theological virtues of faith, hope and love can sustain this kind of intense labor day by day over fifty-three years in joy. These threefold sacred spiritual gifts, stronger than death, guided and empowered Jesse's family, just as they guided and empowered the joy of St. Francis in his dark and tangled hut, and Mary, the mother of Jesus, through the thorns of life and the crucifixion of her son.

Authentic Christian faith is not Pollyanna. It cannot be understood or lived apart from a loving embrace of the cross. It is the victorious love of Christ upon his cross, conquering death for all, and risen in eternal joy, that sustains and keeps us all.

During a public exhibit of John's ikons, a mother, who had brought her handicapped son with her, reported to John that her son was especially drawn to this ikon of Jesse. He seemed able to pull from it what it was written to share.

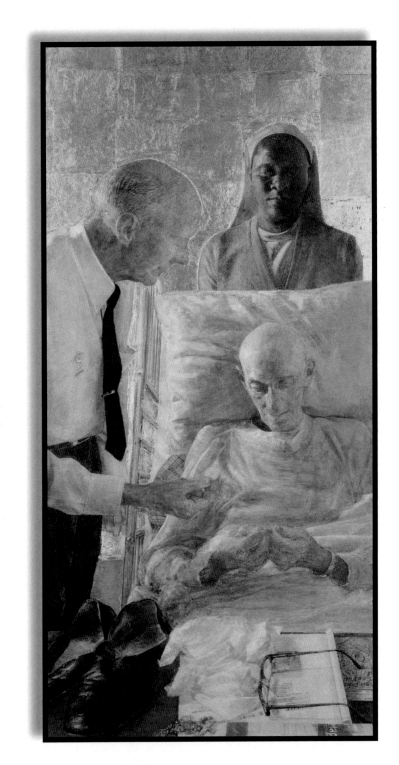

ETERNAL LIFE:
Br. Andrew, CSC
17.5" x 34"
2009

20

ETERNAL LIFE:
BR. ANDREW, CSC

Br. Andrew was Religious Superior of the Brothers of Holy Cross at St. Edward's University. For decades he served the students of St. Edward's as a Professor of English Literature. His favorite course to teach was the poems of T.S. Eliot. He also loved to spend time fishing on the Gulf with friends.

The ikon depicts two Holy Cross religious, Br. Thomas and Sr. Olivia, bringing him Holy Communion at a nursing home in South Austin as he approaches death. The religious brother and sister have brought him the consecrated eucharistic host bearing the body and blood of Christ. It is his *viaticum*, the provision for his ultimate journey into eternal life.

> "The Catholic tradition of giving the Eucharist to the dying ensures that instead of dying alone they die with Christ who promises them eternal life."
>
> Cardinal Javier Lozano Barragan

THE RECORD TAKER:
Br. Jeremiah, CSC
17" x 17"
1991

21

THE RECORD TAKER:
BR. JEREMIAH, CSC

The focus of this ikon are themes from the Gospel of Luke and the Book of Revelation.

"Nothing is covered up that will not be revealed or hidden that will not be known. Whatever you have said in the dark shall be heard in the light, and what you have whispered in private rooms shall be proclaimed upon the housetops."

Luke 12:2-3

Now write what you see, what is and what is to take place hereafter.

Revelation 1:18

Br. Jeremiah Myslewic, a Holy Cross Brother, was also a painter. He and John would go to life-drawing classes together. How he came up with "those pictures" John could never figure out. John describes his art as kind of—primitive, like Grandma Moses. Though they believed in the same things, there was the most incredible disparity of styles between them. The remarkable combination of rich colors in the fire over the mountain in John's ikon Baptism by Fire is a direct copy of Br. Jeremiah's painting, "Fire in the Sky."

John was always impressed by the precise way Br. Jeremiah kept careful written records of everything, entirely unadorned by himself. He wrote in a matter of fact way, a simple, objective record of exactly what was done.

In the final judgment nothing will be hidden, and everything will be made clear. The way Br. Jeremiah kept his record book is a spiritual reminder of the objective record of our lives, of both the good and the ill, that we shall examine dispassionately together with the Lord when we meet him face to face after leaving this world.

FAITH & REASON
17" x 17"
1996

22

THE DIALOGUE OF FAITH & REASON

The woman representing reason is Cleo Cobb McGee, a teacher and John's mother. She approaches things in a very thoughtful and penetrating way. It is as though the seminal idea begins at the back of her head and moves forward to the eyes, with her hands lifting her glasses better to see.

Faith is Mrs. Sandra Soliz, a Hispanic woman. She is open, accepting, contemplative, her hands folded in prayer. In contrast to the dark background, her face is radiated by an interior light to which the face of reason must also turn for its illumination.

***ELDER DRESSED IN WHITE AND
WEARING A GOLDEN CROWN***
17" x 34"
1986

23

ELDER DRESSED IN WHITE & WEARING A GOLDEN CROWN

Reverend Hartness was a Presbyterian minister, retired for a time. He was alone in a solitary room on San Gabriel and 21st St. He stands for good government—manners implacable, quiet consideration, never perhaps his own view—but the whole picture at-large, moral to a "t". He was one of those pioneer figures, stolid, no equivocation, no wandering principles.

It is peculiar to present a heavenly personage in the here and now, a strange paradox sizing up a figure beyond the confines of flesh and blood. But the offsetting association of someone "real" with someone eternal lends itself to happy speculation.

The scripture states, "Surrounding the throne I saw twenty-four other thrones on which twenty-four elders sat, dressed in white garments and with gold crowns on their heads." (*Rev. 4)* The figure must be placed in its ordinary setting and must be so understated that it's reality—its eternal dignity—may only be alluded to. In this way the viewer may comprehend both the plausibility and the unseen glory implied. To tell of the peals of thunder, the flaming torches, the sparkling jasper, the trumpetlike voices, the something that resembled a sea of glass, how could we begin? Better maybe to simply place a minimalist figure to his left to indicate there were more, and in Heaven, we would be greeted with a great deal more.

THE FINAL VOWS OF SISTER MARY THEODORE
34" x 34"
2017

24

THE FINAL VOWS OF SISTER MARY THEODORE

Open to the sky above, in utter resignation, and so, "accepting" and no longer "doing," placing into order wild and woolly nature, full of thorns and survival modes, these were implicit in her statement of sacrifice within the church-like edifice of Enchanted Rock, the sheds of prophecy in the background.

Her attending Monks of the Carmelite Order in the foreground, the orchestrating Priest, the young celebrant holding the standard before the improvised altar, they were blossoming in the atmosphere of her calling, perhaps, even in the utter demolishing of the priests of Baal, and Elijah and fire from Heaven, called.

DREAM OF THE FRIEND
17" x 36"
1987

25

Dream of the Friend

This concluding ikon in this series of meditations is in many ways a summary reflection on a central theme underlying all of them.

While each ikon depicts specific individuals in distinct physical situations, the meaning of the ikon is never reducible to the specifics of the scene depicted. Always the tensions built into the interrelation of the particular individuals and physical context are intended to strike interior sparks illuminating spiritual themes of universal human significance.

In the ikon of the spiritual preparation of Mary as a child, we see her as a little girl on her gentle white pony with her father by its head, passing under thorny mesquite. This is not a meditation just on the preparation of Mary but also on the great diversity of ways across the millennia God acts preveniently to prepare individuals for their unique spiritual vocation in life. The ikon on Peter's repentance is not just about Peter, but also a meditation on what makes authentic repentance or metanoia such a powerful, positive and spiritually healing energy for people in every time and place.

The same is true of this concluding ikon and meditation in our series. It is not just about the particular individuals in the image and the specifics of their tragic family history, it also addresses a matter of universal human importance throughout human history.

What is it that can make "religion" such a beautiful, hopeful, and healing energy for human beings, and what is it that can make it such an angry, terrifying, and destructive force?

Both possibilities are experienced in all the world religions. Can we identify ways of imaging God and the divine will that lead to destructive forms of religious life? And, in contrast, can we identify positive ways of understanding the 'Spirit' and the divine will that lead to religious forms of life which foster humility, tenderness, forgiveness, and reconciliation among human beings? This goal is central to all the ikons and meditations.

A mystical poem by Rumi, a 13th century Muslim, inspired the title, *Dream of the Friend*. The ikon portrays an imagined dream about a beloved friend of John's and her family. All the children were brought up in a Christian household and all suffered terrible things from a perceived angry father's zealous, legalistic, and distorted religious attitude.

In sharing this story, we also caution our readers. We all know from painful family and personal experience that what we perceive in one another in times of anger and intense conflict is often inaccurate. When things get hot and emotional, it becomes difficult to assess with much accuracy the deeper motivations driving our own behaviors. Assessing someone else's accurately is nearly impossible.

In the following account of the children's experience of their father in this family, we must be cautious about passing judgment on him. In heated conflict, when we impute "intentions" or ascribe "character traits" to one another, as in "you always...", things tend to become distorted and get out of control. But whatever the father's actual intentions and hopes may have been, how all of his children experienced him is real, with devasting consequences on the family.

There were two sons and a daughter. The father was a preacher in a church that insisted on literal interpretations of the Bible. The children experienced his teaching of the Bible as extremely authoritarian, black and white, and intolerant of any other possible understandings. What he emphasized is that God's Word is Law and God brooks no dissent. And to disobey that Law as it was preached in his church was to be damned.

They heard only an authoritarian, punishment-oriented, and legalistic view of God, utterly intolerant of other perspectives and devoid of love and mercy. Texts both in the Old and New Testaments emphasizing

God's love and mercy, and biblical warnings that religious legalism is a path to death seemed never to be addressed.

The father's chosen ways of "imaging God" also seemed to rule his understanding of his responsibilities as "head of the family" and how his wife and children should relate to him. Everyone should be subject to his authority and accept his personal interpretations of Scripture as Law. He tolerated no dissent and other views were not permitted.

The eldest son's experience of his father fueled an immense resentment and anger in him. They were in constant head-to-head, emotionally destructive conflict. After years of fighting single-handedly with the father, emotionally destroyed and overwhelmed, he lost all faith in everything, including himself. He took his own life.

The daughter was witness to these head-to-head battles but had no tools to help her brother.

The younger brother had left home and taken a job processing pine logs for firewood. On his way to work, a logging truck hit him. The accident crushed a portion of his skull, causing permanent brain injury.

The dream depicted in the ikon is of the wounded brother's heart-felt return to comfort and console his grieving sister. The dream was the expression of a hopeful prayer in John's mind and heart that the grieving sister would not project her image of her own father's callous and harsh judgments onto God our Father in Heaven. The hope expressed in John's ikon was that some way might be found to open the grieving sister's mind and heart to a vision of God's universal mercy and compassion.

The physical setting is the confluence of the San Juan and Green Rivers in Utah above Lake Powell. The symbolism in the ikon does not focus on the powerful rushing water, but on the action of those waters undermining and cutting away the great sandstone cliffs. This powerful erosional force is here a symbol of death, not of life.

The principal symbolic focus of the ikon, however, is not on the power of water to undermine and topple majestic sandstone cliffs. Rather the ikon focuses on the death of the soul and the corruption of "religious" authority structures. Religion held captive by temporal ways of thinking place a very high priority on physical externals and on control and dominion over others. The lethal force of a zealous, legalistic, power-seeking, distorted, and dishonest religious imagination undermines the life of our souls. Jesus warns his disciples to beware of this life and soul-destroying corruptive force. He calls it "the leaven of the Pharisees." (*Matthew 15:1-12, Matthew 16:6, 16:12; Mark 8:15; Luke 12:1*)

All of the individuals in this story are tragic victims of the leaven of the Pharisees—the father, the dead eldest son, the grieving sister, and the wounded brother appearing in John's imagined dream. Yet the healing power each needs is available, were their hearts and minds to open up to the ever-present redemptive power of the Lamb of God's universal tender mercies.

The sister lies on her side on a rocky ledge, her body curled up almost in a fetal position, in a monastic-looking brown robe and red hood concealing her femininity. She is shrouded in grief and despair, asleep and dreaming.

In the dream, the sister's surviving brother appears as a Christ figure with the healing Light from on High around the gaping wound in his head. The figure rises compassionately over her in a ghostly translucent white robe. The wounded healer stands there in silence, a peaceful, calming presence, his robe extended over her head,

protecting her from the fierce powers of grief.

While this ikon depicts two specific individuals in a southwestern landscape, the theme of their suffering is universal. The same religious violence afflicting them has been and continues to be a dreadful generator of violence and despair across the globe. It is the destroyer, not a defender, of an authentic, healing, and reconciling religious faith.

During the many months John meditated on and crafted this ikon, he found rich and nourishing food for his mind and heart in the writings of Jalal ad-Din Muhammad Rumi, the 13th century Islamic poet, jurist, and theologian. Rumi also had to struggle with the violent undermining powers of corrupted religion in his time and culture. But his spirit was able to transcend these corruptions. Instead he turned the focus of the energies of his heart and mind to what is far more important, the vibrant, healing, and reconciling tasks of authentic religious faith.

Rumi writes,

> Your task is not to seek for love, but merely to seek and find the barriers within yourself that you have built against it... Out beyond our ideas of wrongdoing and rightdoing there is a field. I'll meet you there. When the soul lies down in that grass the world is too full to talk about... and the wound is the place where the light enters you.

In these words of a 13th century Muslim, John encounters the spirit of Jesus. The universal spiritual truth in these words inspired his ikon *Dream of the Friend*. In the yearlong labor of crafting it, he gave witness to "the simple faith that takes delight in any encounter with the Lord, regardless of race, culture, or religion..." (*Pope Francis*, p. 34) It was clear to John that Jesus himself was speaking to him through Rumi's affirmation that the central human task is interior, not exterior. It is not seeking love from others, but rather seeking and finding all the barriers within ourselves that we have built up against it.

This search leads us inevitably to confront our own wounds and brokenness. Our natural biological and psychological tendencies are to run, to flee from brokenness and all its causes. A deep supernatural faith, transcending the ways of this world, leads us on a different path. It empowers forms of religious life that allow "no separation of the friend and your loving," and lead to that mystical place beyond angry words and judgmental ideas of wrongdoing and rightdoing. There the soul can "lie down in that grass the world is too full to talk about... and the wound is the place where the light enters you."

When we foster this spiritual movement forward, we can also experience in truly miraculous ways the positive progression of the three critical movements of the spiritual life: from what is less to what is more important, from the exterior to the interior, and from what passes away to what is eternal.

> O Lord, we are so easily deceived still into expecting from you a kingdom governed according to the laws of this world. Keep our eyes fixed on the triumph of life over death through the mystery of the cross, so that we may grow in a deeper understanding of the power of your law of love over the laws of human expectations, through Christ our Lord.
>
> (*Magnificat*, Holy Week 2020, Palm Sunday Morning Prayer, Vol. 22, No. 1, p. 21)

POSTSCRIPT

If you have found this work helpful and illuminating, John and I need your help. These IKONS have no permanent home yet. Unless they are "on tour" or installed at a temporary exhibit, they are wrapped in paper and stored in John's cramped artist studio or sometimes under a bed.

As you have seen and read, these IKONS represent a lifelong dedicated labor of body, mind, and spirit. A permanent institutional home with sufficient physical and financial resources would preserve them for public viewing and study.

We hope you, or someone you know, will provide practical suggestions to ensure they are available to future generations. Please contact us at wpenn@me.com.

SELECTED BIBLIOGRAPHY

Blowers, Paul M. *Exegesis and Spiritual Pedagogy in Maximus the Confessor*. Indiana: University of Notre Dame Press, 1991.

Bonaventure. *The Soul's Journey Into God, Classics of Western Spirituality*, translation and introduction by Ewert Cousins. New York: Paulist Press, 1978.

Burns, Elizabeth. *The Late Liz, The Autobiography of an Ex-Pagan*. New York: Appleton-Century-Crofts, Inc., 1957.

Catechism of the Catholic Church (CCC), Second Edition, United States Catholic Conference, 1997.

Catherine of Siena. *The Dialogue*, translation and introduction by Suzanne Noffke, O.P., The Classics of Western Spirituality. New York: Paulist Press, 1980.

Christian Prayer, The Liturgy of the Hours. New York: Catholic Book Publishing Co., 1976.

Einstein, Albert. *Out Of My Later Years*. New York: Citadel Press, 1974.

Facing Evil: Confronting the Dreadful Power behind Genocide, Terrorism, and Cruelty. Paul Woodruff and Henry A. Wilmer, editors, Illinois: Open Court, 1988.

Father Arseny, A Cloud of Witnesses, Translated by Vera Bouteneff. New York: St. Vladimir's Seminary Press, 2001.

Father Arseny 1893-1973, Priest, Prisoner, Spiritual Father, Translated by Vera Bouteneff. New York: St. Vladimir's Seminary Press, 1998.

Fitzmeyer, Joseph A. *The Gospel According to Luke, I-IX*, Anchor Bible, Vol. 28A. New York: Doubleday & Co., 1981.

From The Broken Way, A Daring Path to the Abundant Life, 2016, by Ann Morton Voskamp, Zondervan.

Geyer, Ginger Henry. *Art on Board, John Cobb's Panel Paintings Hit the Texas Highways, in Image: Art, Faith, Mystery*, pp. 33-43, Fall 2005, Number 47.

Gottwald, Norman K. *A Light to the Nations, An Introduction to the Old Testament*. New York: Holt Rinehart and Winston, 1969.

Lewis, C.S. *The Great Divorce*. New York: Macmillan Publishing Company, 1946.

Magnificat. Publisher: Pierre-Marie Dumont, POB 834, Yonkers, NY 10702.

McKenzie, John L. *Second Isaiah*, Anchor Bible, Vol. 20. New York: Doubleday & Co., 1968.

Moody, Raymond A. Jr., M.D. *Life After Life, the investigation of a phenomenon—survival of bodily death.* Georgia: Mockingbird Books, 1975.

Morse, Melivin, M.D.. *Closer To The Light: Learning from the Near-Death Experiences of Children.* New York: Random House, 1990.

Mother Teresa, Come Be My Light: The Private Writings of the "Saint of Calcutta", Edited and with Commentary by Brian Kolodiejchuk, M.C.. New York: Doubleday, 2007.

Pope Francis. *Only Love Can Save Us: Letters, Homilies, and Talks of Cardinal Jorge Bergoglio,* Translated by Gerard Seromik. Indiana: Our Sunday Visitor Publishing Division, Our Sunday Visitor, Inc., 2013.

St. Francis of Assisi, Omnibus of Sources. Edited by Marion A. Habig, Third Revised Edition, Illinois: Franciscan Herald Press, 1973.

St. Teresa of Avila, The Collected Works, Volume Two, The Way of Perfection, Meditations on the Song of Songs, The Interior Castle. Translated by Kieran Kavanaugh, O.C.D. and Otilo Rodriguez, O.C.D.. Washington, D.C.: ICS Publications, Institute of Carmelite Studies, 1980.

Spivy, Robert A., and Smith, D. Moody, Jr. *Anatomy of the New Testament: A Guide to Its Structure and Meaning,* Second Edition. New York: Macmillan Publishing Co., 1974.

The New Jerome Biblical Commentary. New Jersey: Prentice-Hall, Inc., 1974.

The Oxford Dictionary of the Christian Church. London: Oxford University Press, 1958.

Uleyn, Arnold. *Is It I, Lord? Pastoral Psychology and the Recognition of Guilt,* translation by Mary Ilford. New York: Holt, Rinehart and Winston, 1969.

ABOUT THE ARTIST

One remembers one's own life and its greatest gifts. Oddly, we rarely realize what the future importance of these gifts might be. So, time distills these memories and places them into a certain relevance. We realize it is not so much the skills we accrued that made the difference, but rather the opportunity someone else gave us that gives our lives meaning.

JOHN COBB, *artist*
Photo by MINOR WILSON

As a young boy in 1961, I attended Texas School of Fine Arts, a private arts school in Austin located at 19th & University. Charles Normann was the teacher there, very portly. He lived in the old Alamo Hotel and swizzled maybe a few at Scholtz's. He was most famous for his "Heroes of the Alamo" series, which were exhibited from time to time at Bradford's Paint Company or at the Country Store Gallery on Lavaca.

The scene at the school was exhilarating: great brown clouds on the papered ceiling, plaster casts of ears and noses, *Arizona Highways* stacked halfway up the walls, postcards of missions, all fodder for painting subjects. The place reeked of gum turpentine, quite possibly the largest fire hazard in all of Austin. It was not to befall this tragedy. Instead it was bulldozed to make room for an education wing of UT.

Attendance there started me on my path and I have pursued it ever since. High school in Corpus Christi brought me into contact with a superb teacher, Grady Waldrop. After high school, a stint of art studies at UT Austin delivered to me a glimpse of the closing heyday of the 60s, Robert Levers, Gibbs Milliken, et. al. The great reach at that point was a foray to Rhode Island School of Design and an extended journey to Europe with a backpack and a Vespa.

I learned so much seeing the museums and doing watercolors in my black sketchbook. I ran out of money and returned to embrace my parents' wishes, pursuing my eventual degree in art from St. Edward's University. I got a Hinson Hazlewood loan and my monthly bill was $33.

What I really discovered while at St. Edward's was that I had no real knowledge of the "Spirit." Oh, maybe Robert Henri's "Art Spirit," but no perception beyond my own understanding. A new concept of believing led to an overwhelming need to be responsible, for myself and for others. My parents' divorce, my own propensity to embrace existentialism (an earlier grappling with Camus' "A Happy Death" in Tetuon, Morocco) led to an underlying dynamic of duress, a complete despair really, an unseen development of a hatred for life and oneself, all because I had no real knowledge of the "Spirit".

The Brothers at St. Ed's revealed to me more positive options. I sensed the possibility of a grounding in a spiritual community. With that, I began this egg tempera series, seeking to generate a sequence of works grounded in ancient traditions and moving towards the here and now and the ever new. My goal is to take what is sacred and to hold it steadfast, while moving forward in ways that no degree of malfeasance could defeat.

ABOUT THE AUTHOR

William Y. Penn, Jr., was born in 1940 in Dallas, Texas. He graduated from Midland High School in Midland, Texas in 1958 and began undergraduate studies at the University of Texas in Austin in the fall of 1958. After a troubled and unsuccessful undergraduate career, in 1962 he left the University without a degree and enlisted in the U.S. Army. He served as a Chaplain's Assistant with the U.S. Army Third Armored Division north of Frankfurt and in 1965 received an honorable European discharge.

WILLIAM Y, PENN, JR., *author*

He remained in Germany for an additional year studying Theology and Scripture at the University of Bonn. In 1966 he returned to the University of Texas at Austin where he completed a B.A. in Philosophy and entered the University's Graduate Program in Philosophy, completing his doctorate in 1976. While ABD (all but dissertation) he taught in an inner city Holy Cross Catholic High School in Akron, Ohio, while completing a dissertation on Soren Kierkegaard. In 1978 he obtained a teaching position in Theology and Philosophy at St. Edward's University in Austin, Texas.

At St. Edward's he also did extensive published research in moral development working with the moral development research programs both at Harvard University and the University of Minnesota. The funding enabling this was provided by the Brothers of Holy Cross at St. Edward's University. This resulted in the development of a new model for teaching undergraduate ethics and a business ethics course in the University's Master of Business Administration program. He also served on the Catholic Diocese of Austin's Theological Commission and taught in the Diocesan Deacon Training Program.

After retiring from St. Edward's in 1999, he taught part-time for five years in the spiritual and intellectual formation program of Los Hermanos y Las Hermanas de Juan Diego in Tulpetlac, Mexico, part of the Mexican Diocese of Ecatepec de Morelos. The Brothers and Sisters in Tulpetlac will always remain for him his *familia mejicana*.

He has three adult children, two sons and a daughter, and two granddaughters. He lives in Austin, Texas, near the University of Texas and within walking distance of his beloved Paulist faith community at St. Austin's Catholic Parish. He also continues to be an avid bicyclist.

He is now eighty years old. Daily he gives thanks to the eternal, merciful Father who never stops blessing him with the necessary strength to continue this wonderful and mysterious physical and spiritual pilgrimage into ever greater goodness, in this life and in the life to come.

ACKNOWLEDGEMENTS

Tina and Jesse Serrano

Ginger Geyer, Austin, Texas

Valley House Gallery, Dallas, Texas

Felder Gallery, San Antonio, Texas

The Magnificat, Yonkers, NY, www.magnificat.com

Mexic-Arte Gallery, Austin, Texas

Cynthia Stone, Treaty Oak Publishers, Inc., Austin, Texas

As I complete the writing of this book and reflect on the many blessings in my life, I wish especially to express my deep personal gratitude to the following persons and institutions who were key guiding and formative stars in my life:

My parents, William Y. Penn and Addilee Lancaster Penn: They were not "helicopter parents" but gave my younger brother Lee and me remarkable freedom, even at an early age, to explore our world and set our own priorities. But we always knew their steadfast love was there for one another and for us. And whenever we faced challenges, we knew they would step forward and provide whatever was needed. From them I also developed a deep love and appreciation for classical music.

My grandmother, Naomi Lancaster: She was an artist and studied under famous artists in the Taos School in Santa Fe and Taos, New Mexico, during the 1940s and 50s. She assisted me in so many ways, both personally and financially. And the introduction she gave me to the fine arts, especially painting and music, brought immeasurable enrichments to my life

Gertrude Behanna, my mother in the faith.

My own family: Lucinda, Gregory, Rebecca, and David, my beloved daughter-in-law, Marsha, and my two beautiful and brilliant granddaughters, Cordy and Chloe.

David Leggett: A lifelong friend and brilliant fellow student at UT. While I was still an undisciplined and unfocused undergraduate, he was the first person ever to suggest to me that my real vocation in life might be as a teacher.

The University of Texas at Austin and its Graduate Program in Philosophy, where, in spite of a very slow start, I gradually developed my love of disciplined academic learning. It was mostly at UT that I developed the knowledge and skills required for my career as a teacher. My Philosophy Professors were remarkably gifted teachers. All had truly important things to teach and "to profess" which came across in their teaching in very lively and living ways.

The Episcopal Theological Seminary of the Southwest, where my mind and heart were first opened to the richness to be found in the study of Theology.

Heinrich Schlier at the University of Bonn, Germany, whose course on St. Paul's Epistle to the Romans first introduced me to the spiritual richness in formal academic studies in Scripture. He was also a significant figure in the Christian resistance to Hitler, as a director of the underground seminary of the Confessing Church in Germany.

The Brothers of Holy Cross who provided the institutional platform and support, apart from which my teaching career would not have been possible.

Larry Kohlberg and Anne Colby at Harvard University and Jim Rest at the University of Minnesota. Their careful empirical research, writings, and personal guidance informed and inspired the fruitfulness of my own research and publications in Moral Development.

Father Joseph Kentenich

The life and teachings of Fr. Joseph Kentenich were a special source of inspiration to me as I was researching and writing these meditations. He was born on November 18, 1885, in Gymnich, Germany and died September 15, 1968, shortly after celebrating Mass in the Adoration Church at Schoenstatt.

Born to a single mom and raised for much of his childhood in an orphanage, his life began with big challenges. He went on to become a Catholic priest and the founder of the many branches of the International Schoenstatt Family Life Movement. Much of his ministry was lived actively sharing in the lives of young people and families in the midst of the ravages of both World War I and World War II.

During the Hitler years, many faithful German Christians, Catholic and Protestant alike, labored openly at great personal risk to strengthen the resistance of believers against Hitler's violent nationalist and anti-semitic strategies undermining the Christian witness of the churches. Fr. Kentenich and his fellow Schoenstatt priests taught and gave widely attended conferences across Germany to achieve this goal. Many doing this kind of work were sent to concentration camps.

When Father Kentenich was sentenced to Dachau, his community considered it a death sentence and arranged a way for him to escape it. To the dismay of many, he rejected it. Instead he chose to pick up the cross set before him and entrusted himself and the future of his religious movement entirely into the hands of God and His Blessed Mother. In faith and in conscience, he chose freely to share in the sufferings of fellow priests, religious, and Catholic laity already imprisoned in the death camp.

While in Dachau, he wrote a prayer book entitled *Heavenward*, which includes these lines from his daily morning consecration prayer:

> "Being strengthened, may I awaken anew your love rekindling...
> Whether failure or success comes our way, our resolve remains your
> love to proclaim."

This is how I begin my morning prayers and focus my day.

Albert Einstein publicly acknowledged the remarkable resistance among faithful German Christians to Hitler's brutal attacks on truth and human freedom. Before the United States entered the war he commented:

> "Being a lover of freedom, when the revolution came in Germany, I looked to the universities to defend it, knowing that they had always boasted of their devotion to the cause of truth; but, no, the universities immediately were silenced. Then I looked to the newspapers whose flaming editorials in days gone by had proclaimed their love of freedom; but they, like the universities, were silenced in a few short weeks...

> "Only the church stood squarely across the path of Hitler's campaign for suppressing truth. I never had any special interest in the church before, but now I feel a great affection and admiration because the church alone has had the courage and persistence to stand for intellectual truth and moral freedom. I am forced thus to confess that what I once despised I now praise unreservedly." (*National Catholic Reporter*, March 23, 1979, p. 26)

Alan and Tricia Graham

Founders of Mobile Loaves and Fishes and Community First, living embodiments of the Gospel *con carne* in Austin, Texas. Their steadfast faith, unrelenting persistence, clear-headed and realistic thinking have demonstrated just how much can be accomplished to feed the hungry and shelter the homeless in modern urban environments. Mobile Loaves and Fishes has generated a fleet of trucks from church commissaries going into the streets to feed the hungry every day. Community First has a 51-acre development providing hundreds of homes and genuine community for the homeless, a broad outreach that includes all levels of society. It is truly a Christian revolution in goodness taking place in Austin, with a growing impact on other cities across the nation. My involvement in their programs greatly increased my sensitivity to the needs of the homeless and practical ways of meeting them.

Hermanos y Hermanas de Juan Diego, Tulpetlac, Mexico

A modern mendicant Franciscan community in Tulpetlac Mexico in the Catholic Diocese of Ecatepec Morelos. Their principal mission is empowering the poor to evangelize the poor in Mexico. The five-year period of my teaching part-time in their intellectual and spiritual formation program greatly enhanced my understanding not only of the needs of the poor but also of their remarkable generosity and giftedness. During those five years, I developed a deeper and more intimate understanding of the Franciscan Theologian St. Bonaventure and the three critical movements in the spiritual life that I drew upon repeatedly in these meditations.